IDENTITY

Unveiling Your True Self Beyond Performance, Approval, and External Labels

ALowe McCants

Published by ALowe McCants / Trillion $$$ Lady

Birmingham, Alabama

alowemerch.com • itsalowe.com

First Edition, 2026

Printed in the United States of America

ISBN: 979-8-9881369-6-5

IDENTITY is the first book in the Four I's series:

Identity • Intention • Implementation • Increase

Because before God changes what you do, He settles who you are.

For the one who has been wearing someone else's name.

For Matt — Future Hall of Fame Coach!! Thank you for choosing all of me, every day. You have stood with me through every season, and I am grateful to have you as my partner in this life. I Love you, Coach!

Sam — You are my joy. I am so proud to be your mother. You are one of the greats. You will do AMAZING things. I am happy to see all you will become! Mommie Loves You!!

For my father — Your pulpit taught me the Word. You led me to the Father. You taught me to study the Word for myself. You introduced me to the Hebrew language, God's language, and showed me to never think I have Him figured out. There is always more. I love you.

For my mother —My first example of a praying woman. Classy. Creative. Charismatic. You have always inspired me to get it done. Now you are a rapping grandma inspiring the world with your songs. I am proud to call you My Mom. Thank you for your love and your support. I love you.

And for you — the one who picked up this book. It was not an accident.

TABLE OF CONTENTS

The label on your cover was never yours to fill in.

A NOTE BEFORE WE BEGIN

This book was born from obedience. I heard God tell me to start going live every morning M-F, at 6:15 am CST to encourage others about the 4 I's: Identity, Intention, Implementation, and Increase. At first I wasn't sure that I had heard Him but I got started. For the entire first quarter I spoke on Identity and from those notes and study came this book.

Wheww... This book asked me to look in a mirror. Not the kind in your bathroom that shows you what you look like on the outside, but the kind that shows you who you've been, what you've believed about yourself, and the gap between that version and who God always said you were.

That kind of mirror is uncomfortable. And for a long time, I avoided it.

I want you to understand where I come from, because it matters for where this book goes.

On my father's side, I come from a lineage of men who moved people. My grandfather J.L. Lowe was a longtime jazz musician and educator. Jazz, which means he understood that the notes you do not play are just as important as the ones you do. He understood space, timing, and the courage it takes to improvise when the sheet music runs out.

My uncle Sammy Lowe carries that same gift, a musician and composer whose fingerprints are on some of the greatest music you have ever heard. I promise. My grandmother Roberta became the first Black female chiropractor in the state of Alabama, which means she walked into rooms that were not expecting her and changed what was possible just by being there. And my father built a megachurch, a man who has spent his life helping people hear what God is saying over the noise of everything else.

On my mother's side, I come from people who found their way without a map. My grandfather L.B. Bruce drove buses across this nation before GPS existed. Let that land for a second. He navigated roads, routes, and terrain without a system telling him where to go. He had to know the road himself. He had to trust his own sense of direction. He had to keep moving even when the path was not clearly marked. My grandmother Vivian was an educator. And my mother is one of the top Insurance Agents in the country, a woman who built something real through discipline, strategy, and showing up when it would have been easier not to.

Greatness surrounded me in every direction.

And somehow, in the middle of all of that, I completely lost myself.

Not because my family failed me. They didn't. But legacy can be a gift and a weight at the same time. When you grow up surrounded by people who seem to know exactly who they are and where they are going, it is easy to quietly absorb the pressure to match it.

And then life started moving.

I met Matt McCants in the theater hallways at UAB. Back then, we were just two college students trying to figure it out. Did you know that in 2011, we were voted UAB Theatre's Cutest Couple? We graduated that same year and then 2012 came, and everything shifted.

He was drafted to the New York Giants. The following year, we got married, and just like that, life picked up speed. New York. Oakland. Cleveland. Chicago. Cleveland. St.Louis. Back to Birmingham, now with Sam and even at 9 Years old. I know even He is destined for Great and remarkable things.

Whew we have done a lot in these 13 years. New cities. New environments. New expectations. And here is what nobody tells you.

When life starts moving fast, you can look like you are walking in purpose while quietly losing yourself in the process. I was showing up. I was supporting. I was adjusting. I was moving. But I still did not know who I was.

And when you do not know who you are, you will attach yourself to roles, titles, and seasons, hoping one of them will answer the question for you.

But none of them did.

I knew all the church language. I had grown up in the Word. I could quote scriptures and say all the right things. But deep down, when nobody was watching, I did not know who I was apart from what I did, who I was related to, or what role I was playing at any given moment.

Being a Football Wife gave me a title. Being in rooms full of high achievers gave me a standard to perform against. But none of it gave me identity.

And a person who does not know who they are will fill that emptiness with something. What I filled it with, for a season, was armor. Toughness. Walls. A version of strength that was really just fear with better posture.

But God.

I love those two words. Because they mean the story does not end where it looked like it would. God began to work on me in ways I did not ask for and did not always appreciate. He started stripping things, roles, relationships, images, until all that was left was me and Him. And in that quiet, uncomfortable, sometimes painful process, He showed me something I had never been able to see when I was busy performing.

He showed me who He made me to be. Not the pastor's daughter. Not the Football wife. Not Extra. Not the woman in someone else's shadow. Just me. ALowe. His daughter. His workmanship. His purpose walking around in a human body.

And that changed everything.

I wrote my first book, The Triumph Playbook, about overcoming darkness. This book is the natural next chapter. Because once you get up, once you overcome, once you decide to stop letting pain and pressure define your story.... you still have to answer the question of who you are. You still have to figure out what you are standing on.

This book is that answer.

Before we get started, a few things I want you to know:

First — this is a safe space. I am going to be real with you, and I am asking you to be real with yourself. Some chapters will make you uncomfortable. Some might make you cry. Some might make you mad. That is okay. Discomfort is usually a sign that God is working on something.

Second — write in this book. There are writing lines at the end of every chapter. Do not skip them. This is a working document between you and God. Your handwriting belongs in these pages.

Third — the Hebrew word studies are not there to impress anyone. They are there because when you see what a word actually means in the language God first used, something shifts. I will keep it short and plain. Just enough to let the Word open up for you.

Fourth — pray the prayers out loud. Not because God needs the volume. Because you need to hear yourself agree with truth.

The label on your cover was never yours to fill in. Let's find out whose handwriting it actually is.

With love and truth,
ALowe McCants

PART ONE

THE LABEL
PROBLEM

---

*"Before God can rename you, you have to look at the names
you have been wearing."*

CHAPTER 1

What's Your Name?

The labels we wear, and how they got there

> **Have you ever walked into a room and realized that before you even opened your mouth, someone had already decided who you were?**

They looked at what you were wearing. They heard your last name. They saw who you walked in with, or who you did not walk in with. They noticed what neighborhood you came from, what church you attend, what you do for a living, or what you used to doand before you ever introduced yourself, a verdict was already in.

That is a label.

And the hard truth, honey, is that most of us have been carrying labels for so long that we have forgotten we are wearing them.

We do not think of them as labels anymore. We think of them as facts. We think of them as personality. We think of them as just the way we are. We say things like: "That's just how I am." Or: "I have always been like this." Or: "I can't help it, that's just me."

But what if it is not you?

What if some of the most defining "facts" you believe about yourself are actually just labels, placed on you by other people, by painful seasons, by a culture that reduced you to your most visible quality, or by your own voice on your worst day?

What if the name you have been answering to was never yours to begin with?

The Label We All Wear

Think about a price tag on a piece of clothing. It tells you the value someone assigned. It tells you what someone decided this item is worth. But the tag is not the garment. The tag can be wrong. The tag can undervalue what it is attached to. The tag can say bargain bin when the item belongs in a museum.

The tag is not the truth. It is someone's assignment of worth based on what they could see from where they were standing.

Now think about your life. Think about the invisible tags you carry.

Some of them were given in childhood. You were the smart one, the responsible one, the wild one, the difficult one. You were the child who had to be strong because someone else in the family needed help. You were the one told you were too much, or not enough, or both in the same week. You were the kid who learned early that approval came when you performed and disappeared when you did not.

Some of your labels were given by loss. You became the woman who lost a baby. The man who lost his business. The person who went through the divorce. The one whose family fell apart. When something painful happens, it has a way of becoming your identifier, your whole story collapsed into one defining event.

Some labels were given by comparison. In a room full of gifted, beautiful, accomplished people, you got quiet. You measured. You concluded. And the conclusion was not kind. You walked away from that comparison with a label that said: not enough.

And some, some of the most dangerous ones, were given by success. Wheww... You know the labels that sound good from the outside but still cage you. The one who has it all together. The strong one. The one who never needs anything. The one people lean on but no one ever thinks to check on. Because strength became your label, and now you do not know how to be anything else even when you are falling apart inside.

In the Beginning, God Did the Naming

Here is something I want you to see in Scripture that most people rush past. This right here is about to free about 12 of y'all holding this book.

In the second chapter of Genesis, God brings every creature before Adam and tells him to name them. Whatever Adam called each living creature, that was its name. Adam had naming authority over creation.

> *"Out of the ground the Lord God formed every beast of the field and every bird of the air, and brought them to Adam to see what he would call them. And whatever Adam called each living creature, that was its name."* — **Genesis 2:19 (NKJV)**

But here is what I want you to notice. God gave Adam authority to name the animals. He gave him authority to tend the garden and cultivate the earth. But the one thing Adam was never handed authority over?

His own name.

God named Adam. Not Adam. God.

The name Adam comes from the Hebrew word 'adamah,' which means ground, earth, red soil. God named him from what He made him from. The name carried the identity. And the identity came from the Maker, not from the made.

And yet here we are, thousands of years later, letting everything and everyone except the Maker write our names.

We let wounds write our names. We let relationships write our names. We let seasons of failure write our names, and seasons of success write our names, and the culture writes our names, and sometimes, on the hardest days, we write our own names in ink made entirely from our worst moments.

But you were never given the pen. Only God was.

THE WORD: **Shem (SHAYM)**

Name, but in Hebrew, far more than a label. A name was an identity declaration. It described character, destiny, and nature.

When God changed someone's name in the Bible, He was not just updating their paperwork. He was rewriting their entire trajectory. When Abram became Abraham. When Jacob became Israel. When Simon became Peter. These were not rebranding exercises. These were identity transformations.

God knew something we have forgotten: the name you carry shapes the life you live.

If your name is "not enough," you will live small. If your name is "broken," you will protect brokenness as your home base. If your name is "overlooked," you will shrink in every room that might notice you, because deep down you have accepted that invisible is just what you are.

The name we answer to is the life we live.

So what name have you been answering to?

The Labels That Sound Like Identity But Are Not

Some of the labels we carry hardest are the ones that are not entirely false. They are not outright lies. They are incomplete truths that got promoted to full identity.

You may genuinely be a strong person. But strength is not your identity, it is a gift God placed in you for specific purposes. When strength becomes your identity, you cannot be weak. You cannot need anything. You cannot receive help. Because if you are not strong, you do not know who you are.

You may genuinely be gifted. But gifting is not your identity, it is an expression of something God placed in you for others. When gifting becomes your identity, your worth lives and dies on how the gift is received. A season of low visibility, a project that does not land, a moment when the gift feels dry, and suddenly you do not know who you are.

You may genuinely have been through something hard. But your testimony is not your identity, it is the story of what God did in and through a specific season. When what happened to you becomes your identity, the healing feels like a threat. Because if you are not defined by that pain anymore, who are you?

These labels are sneaky precisely because they are rooted in something real. And the sneakiest ones are not the dramatic ones. They are the ones that sound almost harmless. The ones you laughed along with. I know because I carried one for years.

One of my labels was Blonde.

Not because I dyed my hair that color. Because I asked questions.

Somewhere along the way, asking questions stopped being curiosity and started being a diagnosis. People laughed. Or they answered with that particular tone, the patient one, the slightly condescending one, the one that says *we expected this from you*. And I never argued. I just quietly agreed.

I internalized it so completely that I stopped seeing myself as inquisitive. I stopped calling it learning. I told myself my mind just worked slower than other people's. And I carried that into decisions that had consequences I could not fully see at the time.

I did not go after the challenging classes in college. Not because I could not have passed them. Because I had already decided I was not smart enough to try. I had already talked myself out of rooms I had every right to walk into, because of a label I picked up from other people's laughter and made into a ceiling for my own life.

I want you to feel the weight of that. A word. A laugh. A tone. And a whole corridor of doors I stopped even trying to open.

Now. If you have read this far, if you have read through the Hebrew word studies, the theological unpacking, the scriptural depth of what we have covered together, I need you to understand something. The hundreds of people I have coached, the lives that have been changed, the book you are holding in your hands right now, all of it exists because at some point I had to look at that label and say: that is not my name.

Blonde was a description someone else made. Inquisitive is who God designed me to be. And a person who asks questions, who wants to understand things at the root level, who will not stop digging until the truth comes clear, that is not a liability. That is exactly the kind of mind God uses to help other people get free.

The label almost cost me everything God had prepared for the real version of me.

(I wonder what yours has been costing you.)

This is the subtle damage that labels do. They take something real and make it total. They take a part of you and call it all of you.

You are more than the strongest thing about you. You are more than the most broken thing about you. You are more than the most impressive thing about you.

You are a full human being, made in the image of God, carrying a depth and a design that no single label can contain.

What God Calls You Is the Beginning

The problem is not that labels exist. Labels are everywhere and they always will be. People will always have opinions. Seasons will always try to define you. Culture will always want to reduce you to your most visible quality.

The problem is when we do not have a stronger name to return to.

When you know what God calls you, when that is settled so deep in your spirit that no other voice can overwrite it, labels lose their power. They can come. They can be loud. They can come from people you love and people you respected and people whose opinion you gave too much weight for too long. They can come from your own mouth on your worst days.

And you can look at every single one of them and say: that is not my name.

Because you know what your name is.

That is what this book is about. Not helping you build a better self-image through positive thinking. Not teaching you to ignore the hard things in your story. But helping you discover, or return to, the name that was written over you before you were born, by the only One who had the authority to write it.

God saw you before anyone else did. He named you before anyone else could. And everything He said is still true, regardless of what got written on top of it.

We are going to spend this book peeling back the layers. Not to erase your story. But to find what was underneath it all along.

Let's begin.

> *The name **you** answer to is the life **you** live. But you were never given the pen. Only God was.*

THE LABEL EXCHANGE

The Label Says...	God Says...
You are defined by what happened to you.	You are designed by the One who was there before it happened.
Your worth is tied to what you produce.	Your worth was established before you produced anything.
The loudest voice in the room wrote your name.	The One who formed you in the womb wrote your name first.
You are the sum of your labels.	You are the image of God. No label can contain that.
That's just who you are.	That is who you have been agreeing with. You can change the agreement.

Take your time with these. Write honestly. This is your book.

1. Write down every label you currently carry — the ones people gave you, the ones your history gave you, and the ones you gave yourself. Don't edit. Just name them.

2. For each label you wrote down — where did it come from? Who gave it to you? When did you start agreeing with it?

3. Which label has cost you the most? How has agreeing with it shaped your decisions, your relationships, or the way you show up in rooms?

Use this space. Write without filter.

"Fear not, for I have redeemed you; I have called you by your name; you are Mine."

— Isaiah 43:1 (NKJV)

Ready to Talk to God? Pray this...

Father,

I come to You today with open hands and an honest heart. I have been carrying names that You never gave me. I have been answering to labels that were written over me by pain, by people, by my own worst moments, and I have let those labels become my truth. Forgive me for giving other voices more authority than Yours. Today I ask You to begin showing me what You wrote over me before anyone else had a pen. I am ready to know my real name. In Jesus' name, Amen.

CHAPTER 2

The First Label Theft

How it all started in a garden... and why it is still happening to you

> *What if the identity crisis you are living in right now did not start with you, and the enemy has been running the exact same play since the very beginning?*

I need to take you back to a garden.

Not because this is a history lesson. But because the root of every label problem you have ever experienced is buried in a scene that happened before any of us arrived, and until we understand what happened there, we will keep fighting the symptoms without ever addressing the source.

So we are going back to Genesis 3. Back to the beginning of the identity crisis. And I want you to look at it closely, because what the enemy did there is exactly what he is doing to you right now.

Before the Theft: What Identity Looked Like

Before we get to what went wrong, you need to understand what went right.

In the first two chapters of Genesis, before any sin entered the story, Adam and Eve walked this earth in a state that most of us have never personally experienced. They were naked and unashamed. Fully exposed. Fully known. Nothing hidden, nothing performed, nothing managed.

Just two people in perfect communion with the God who made them.

There was no second-guessing. No measuring yourself against the other person in the garden. No rehearsing how you would be perceived before you spoke. No wondering if you were enough or too much. No building walls to protect yourself from being seen. No armor. No performance. No labels at all.

Just being.

That is what settled identity looks like. Not arrogance. Not perfection. Just a deep, unshakeable knowing of who you are and whose you are, so solid that you do not need anything external to confirm it, and you are not threatened by anything external that tries to deny it.

That is what God designed for us. That is the original condition.

And then the enemy showed up.

THE WORD: **'Arom (ah-ROME)**

Naked — but in Genesis 2, it meant freedom, not shame.

The same nakedness that was freedom before the fall became the source of shame after it. An identity crisis does not change what you are. It changes how you see yourself.

The Oldest Weapon in the Enemy's Arsenal

Pay very close attention to how the enemy approached this, because his strategy in Genesis 3 is his strategy today. He has not updated the playbook in thousands of

years. He does not need to. The same move keeps
working.

He did not come in with a direct attack. He did not show
up with a weapon. He came with something much more
dangerous.

He came with a question.

> *"Has God indeed said, 'You shall not eat of every tree
> of the garden'?"* — **Genesis 3:1 (NKJV)**

"Has God indeed said...?" That is the entire weapon. A
question. A seed of doubt planted right at the root of what
they knew to be true about God and about themselves.

Notice what he did not do. He did not tell them an obvious
lie. He took something true and twisted it just enough to
make Eve wonder whether she had heard God correctly.
Whether God had been fully honest with her. Whether
maybe, just maybe, there was something she was missing
out on.

He turned her attention from what God had given to what
God had withheld. And in that turning, everything
changed.

The enemy has been asking the same question over you
ever since.

He whispers: Has God really said you are chosen? Has
God really said you have purpose? Has God really said
that past doesn't define you? Because look at your track
record. Look at how you have failed. Look at the labels
other people have placed on you, are you really sure God
sees something different?

And because we have not settled the question of our identity in Christ, those whispers have power over us.

The enemy attacks identity before he attacks anything else. Because when identity falls, everything else follows on its own. A person who does not know who they are will make decisions rooted in fear instead of faith. They will shrink in moments they should be bold. They will say yes to things that are wrong for them because they do not have the foundation to say no.

> *The enemy attacks identity before he attacks anything else. Because when identity falls, everything else follows.*

The Moment Everything Changed

Genesis 3:7 says this: Then the eyes of both of them were opened, and they realized they were naked.

The enemy had told them their eyes would be opened, and he was not entirely wrong. But what they saw when they looked at themselves was not the greatness he had implied. What they saw was nakedness. Exposure. Vulnerability. And for the first time in human history, they experienced something that had never existed in the human story before.

Shame.

Now I need to stop here and make a distinction that I believe could change your life, because most people lump guilt and shame together and they are not the same thing at all.

Guilt says: I did something wrong.

Shame says: I am something wrong.

Guilt is about behavior. Shame is about identity. Guilt can lead to repentance, to correction, to restoration. Shame leads somewhere else entirely. Shame leads to hiding.

The very first thing Adam and Eve did when shame entered was reach for fig leaves. They constructed a version of themselves that would be acceptable, or at least would not expose the unacceptable parts. And then when they heard God walking in the garden, they hid from His presence.

They hid from God.

The same two people who had walked in perfect, open, unguarded communion with their Creator now ran from His presence. Because shame does not just make you hide from people. It makes you hide from God. It makes you build a version of yourself to show the world while the real you stays buried underneath the fig leaves, terrified of being fully seen.

THE WORD: **Bosh (BOSH)**
Shame — to be put to shame, to fail, to be disappointed.
The first emotional response after the fall was shame, bosh. The enemy's goal was never just to get them to eat the fruit. It was to introduce shame, which would drive them into hiding and make them think they had to earn their way back to God.

The Fig Leaves We Are Still Wearing

Fig leaves in the ancient garden were a desperate, inadequate attempt to cover what shame had exposed. They grabbed what was available and made a covering. It was flimsy. It was temporary. It was completely insufficient for what they were trying to hide. But it felt like something. It felt like control over a situation that had just spun out of control.

Modern fig leaves look different, but the function is identical.

We build them out of achievement. If I accomplish enough, produce enough, prove enough, no one will see what I feel underneath. The performance becomes the cover.

We build them out of personalities we craft for specific rooms. The church version. The work version. The family version. The social media version. Each one a leaf, carefully placed to cover the place we are most afraid of being seen.

We build them out of busyness. When you are always moving, always serving, always doing, no one gets close enough to ask how you are actually doing. Because if they asked, and you answered honestly, the fig leaves might fall.

We build them out of toughness. There was a season in my own life when I wore sharpness like a coat of armor. I was not difficult by accident. I was building a barrier. Because if no one could get close, no one could hurt me. What I called strength was really just fig leaves dressed up in confidence.

None of these things are sustainable. None of them actually cover what they are trying to hide. And every one of them costs us the very thing we need most: the freedom to be fully known and fully loved anyway.

Because here is the thing about fig leaves: while you are busy wearing them, you cannot receive what God is trying to give you. You cannot receive healing in the places you are hiding. You cannot receive restoration for what you will not acknowledge. You cannot receive the new name if you are too busy managing the old one.

God's First Response: Not Judgment. A Question.

This is the part of the Genesis 3 story that gives me chills every time I read it. When God came looking for Adam and Eve, His first response was not a verdict. It was not a list of everything they had done wrong. It was not condemnation.

It was a question.

> *"Then the Lord God called to Adam and said to him, "Where are you?""* — **Genesis 3:9 (NKJV)**

God is omniscient. He knew exactly where Adam was. He did not need the information. But Adam needed something that only the question could give him: an invitation to come out of hiding.

God was not approaching with a weapon. He was approaching with an open door. Come out. Tell Me where you are. Stop hiding behind what you constructed to cover yourself. I already know. I see you anyway. And I am still here.

Adam's answer is one of the most honest and heartbreaking moments in all of Scripture. He said: I heard You in the garden, and I was afraid because I was naked, so I hid.

I was afraid. I was naked. I hid. That is the anatomy of shame. Fear of exposure, leading to concealment.

And God's response was not to condemn Adam for the nakedness. God's response was to begin the process of covering him, not with fig leaves, but with something real and lasting. Genesis 3:21 tells us that God Himself made garments of skin and clothed them.

The covering God provides is always more substantial than the covering we construct for ourselves. And it always costs something He paid, not something we owe.

THE WORD: **Ayeka (ay-YEH-kah)**

Where are you? — One single word in Hebrew. God's question to Adam.

It was not a question seeking information. It was an invitation: Come out. Stop hiding. I am not asking because I lost you. I am asking because you need to recognize where you have gone.

Why This Matters for Your Labels

Every false label you are wearing traces back to this moment. Every name someone gave you that God never authorized. Every definition you absorbed from pain, from comparison, from failure, from a culture that did not know what you were made from. All of it has the same source: the enemy's original strategy to get you to question what God said and to hide from the truth of who you actually are.

The enemy did not get creative. He got effective. And he has been running the same play ever since.

He comes not with a declaration but with a question. Not "You are worthless" that is too obvious. He comes with: "Are you sure God really made you for something significant?" "Do you really think those gifts are real?" "Look at your past, do you honestly think God sees something good when He looks at you?"

And when we agree with those questions, even partially, even quietly, we reach for fig leaves. We start performing. We start managing what people see. We start hiding the real version and showing the curated one.

And we end up exactly where Adam and Eve did, covered, but not healed. Present, but not free. Known by name, but hiding from the God who is calling us out.

The good news, and there is very good news, is that God is still asking the same question He asked in that garden.

Where are you?

Not because He lost you. Because He wants you to come out.

He is not standing at the edge of the garden with a list of everything that went wrong. He is standing there with the same posture He always had: Come. Be known. Be seen. Let Me show you who you actually are when the fig leaves come off.

Come out of hiding. Your real name is waiting.

1. What are your modern fig leaves — the things you use to cover the parts of yourself you are most afraid of being seen? Be specific and honest.

2. What has the enemy been whispering to you about your identity? Write out the specific doubts. Then next to each one, write what you know God's Word actually says.

3. Guilt says I did something wrong. Shame says I am something wrong. Which one have you been living under? How has it shown up in how you approach God?

PRAY THIS

Father,

I choose to come to You the way Adam and Eve should have come, out of hiding, out in the open, choosing honesty over concealment.I acknowledge that I have let shame drive me away from You instead of toward You. I have built fig leaves and called them strength. I have hidden the real version of myself and presented the managed one.Today I step out. I bring You what I actually am, not what I wish I were, not what I perform for everyone else. The real me.And I trust that You already knew. And that You are still here.Heal the shame. Show me who I am beneath it.In Jesus' name, Amen.

PART TWO

WHAT GOD ACTUALLY WROTE

"Before anyone else had a pen, God had already written the truest thing about you."

CHAPTER 3

Written Before You Were Born

Chosen, specific, intentional, your existence was planned

> ***What would change about how you walk through this week if you genuinely believed that God chose you, not for what you could do, but simply because He wanted you?***

Stay with me on that question. Do not rush past it.

Because I have found that most people, if they are honest, have a very complicated relationship with the idea of being chosen. We hear it in church. We say amen when the pastor preaches it. We write it on our vision boards and post it on our social media. But somewhere between the Sunday morning declaration and the Monday morning mirror, we stop fully believing it.

We believe it in theory. We struggle to live it in practice.

And I think the reason is this: we are trying to receive the truth of being chosen while still operating under labels that tell us we are not.

You cannot fully receive "You are chosen" when you are still secretly agreeing with "You are not enough." Those two things cannot occupy the same foundation. One has to become louder than the other. And in this chapter, we are going to make sure the right one wins.

Before the Foundation of the World

I want to read you one of the most staggering sentences in all of Scripture. And I need you to read it slowly, because we have become so familiar with it that we have lost the weight of it.

> *"He chose us in Him before the foundation of the world, that we should be holy and without blame before Him in love, having predestined us to adoption as sons by Jesus Christ to Himself, according to the good pleasure of His will."* — Ephesians 1:4-5 (NKJV)

Before the foundation of the world.

Before time began. Before creation existed. Before there was a universe to speak of, before there was a you to speak of, God chose you. Not generally. Not as part of some vague category of humans. You. Specifically. Intentionally.

He chose you before you had a name. Before you had a face. Before you had a history, before you had done anything good or bad, before you had any track record to base the decision on. He chose you.

Now I know someone reading this is about to say: that sounds nice, but I was not exactly a planned pregnancy. My parents were not expecting me. My family was not ready for me. My arrival was not exactly celebrated. How does "chosen before the foundation of the world" fit with the reality of how I got here?

God does not need anyone's cooperation to accomplish His purposes. He did not need your parents to plan you in order for Him to choose you. The choosing happened in eternity past, and the choosing is sovereign. It is not subject to human plans or human failures or human readiness.

You were not a surprise to God. Even if you were a surprise to everyone else.

THE WORD: **Yada (yah-DAH)**

To know intimately — not surface knowledge, but deep, personal, covenant knowing.

Jeremiah 1:5 says God 'knew' Jeremiah before He formed him in the womb. That word is yada — the same word used for the most intimate kind of knowing. God did not know of you. He knew you.

The Sequence That Changes Everything

> *"Before I formed you in the womb I knew you; before you were born I sanctified you; I ordained you a prophet to the nations."* — Jeremiah 1:5 (NKJV)

I want you to see the sequence in that verse, because the order is everything.

First He knew Jeremiah. Then He set him apart. Then He appointed him to his assignment.

The knowing came before the setting apart. The setting apart came before the appointment. Which means identity always precedes purpose. Who you are in God always comes before what you do for God.

So many of us have been running this backward. We have been trying to find our identity through our purpose, trying to figure out who we are by doing things and seeing what sticks, by achieving things and measuring our worth by the results, by performing roles and trying to feel our way into an identity through the performance.

But that is backwards. You cannot find your identity through your assignment. Your assignment flows from your identity.

My grandfather L.B. Bruce drove routes across this country that no GPS had ever mapped. He knew the road because he had studied it, learned it, prepared for it. He did not arrive at a destination and then figure out who he was. He knew who he was long before the first trip began. The knowing came first.

That is the order God uses. The knowing comes first. Everything else follows.

THE WORD: **Qadash (kah-DAHSH)**

To set apart, to make holy, to consecrate for a specific purpose.

Before Jeremiah said a word, before he made a single choice, God had already qadash'd him. The setting apart came before the living. You were set apart before you knew there was anything to be set apart for.

Chosen With Full Knowledge

Here is the part of this truth that I need you to sit inside for a moment, because I think it is the part that actually changes things at the level of daily life.

God did not choose you based on an idealized version of who you might become. He did not choose you thinking you would be perfect and then get surprised by your failures. He is omniscient. He knew. He knew about the seasons you would struggle in. He knew about the mistakes you would make. He knew about the ways you would fall and fail and fall again. He knew about the mean season, the broken season, the hiding season. He knew about the things you are most ashamed of.

And He chose you anyway.

Not in spite of those things exactly, but with full knowledge of them. The choosing happened in eternity past, with complete information. God looked at the whole story, beginning, middle, end, all the messy parts in between, and said: I choose her. I choose him. This is the one I want.

If that does not make you stop and breathe for a moment, read it again.

You are chosen. Specifically. Intentionally. With full knowledge. Before the foundation of the world.

That is your identity. Not your worst season. Not your greatest achievement. Not your title or your lineage or your performance or the labels the world gave you. Before any of that existed, you were chosen.

Chosen vs. Convenient

Some of us have experienced a counterfeit version of being chosen. We have been in relationships, romantic, professional, ministerial, where someone chose us, but what they were really doing was selecting us for what we could offer them. They chose us because we were useful.

That is not chosen. That is convenient.

And when people who have experienced convenient hear the language of being chosen by God, they sometimes receive it through the filter of what they know. They think: okay, God chose me because He needs me to do something.

But that is not how God chooses.

God does not need you. Let that sit for a moment. He is God. He could accomplish everything He wants to accomplish without you. He is not scrambling to fill positions.

He chose you because He wanted you. Not for what you could offer Him. For who you are to Him.

Ephesians 1:4 says He chose us to be holy and without blame before Him in love. The choosing was first about relationship, about intimacy, about who we would be in His presence. The assignment came after the love. The purpose flowed from the belonging.

You are not convenient. You are chosen. There is a world of difference between those two things.

> ***You*** *are not convenient.* ***You*** *are chosen. The choosing happened in eternity past, with full knowledge, and it has not changed.*

Take your time with these. Write honestly. This is your book.

1. Have you ever been "convenient" to someone rather than truly chosen? How has that experience shaped the way you receive God's choosing of you?

2. God chose you with full knowledge of everything you are and everything you have done. What specifically do you struggle to believe He knew and chose you anyway?

3. The sequence is: identity first, assignment second. Where have you been trying to find your identity through your purpose instead of receiving it before your purpose?

Write a response to this truth: God chose you before you were born, with full knowledge of everything you are. What does that change?

"You did not choose Me, but I chose you and appointed you that you should go and bear fruit."

— John 15:16 (NKJV)

PRAY THIS

Father,

I want to receive this today in a way I may never have fully received it before. You chose me. Not because You needed me. Not because I earned it. Not because I performed well enough or came from the right background or had the right track record. You chose me because You wanted me. Before the foundation of the world, with full knowledge of everything I am and everything I am not, You chose me. Heal the places in me that were formed by being treated as convenient rather than chosen. Let me know the difference between how people have chosen and how You choose. I receive the truth of being chosen today. Not as a nice idea. As the foundation I stand on. In Jesus' name, Amen.

CHAPTER 4

Your Original Design

You are not a mistake, a copy, or a lesser version — you are God's poem

---

> **Have you ever looked at your life and felt like you were someone else's rough draft?**

Like you were the version God made before He figured out what He was really doing. Like you came out close to the intention but not quite there. Like somewhere out there is the real version of what you were supposed to be, and the version standing in the mirror is just a decent approximation.

If that thought has ever crossed your mind, even once, even quietly, I want to deal with it right now. Because it is one of the most effective lies the enemy tells.

You are not a rough draft.

You are not an approximation. You are not a lesser version of the person you were supposed to be. You are not random. You are not assembled by accident.

You are crafted.

The Word That Should Stop You Cold

> *"For we are His workmanship, created in Christ Jesus for good works, which God prepared beforehand that we should walk in them."* — **Ephesians 2:10 (NKJV)**

The Greek word Paul used is poiema. Say it out loud. Poiema.

Poiema is the word from which we get our English word poem. It means a work of art. A masterpiece. Something that was made with creative intentionality, with skill, with attention to every detail, with a vision in the maker's mind that was being worked out through the making.

When Paul says we are God's poiema, he is not saying we were assembled on an assembly line. He is saying we were crafted, the way an artist crafts something. With care. With purpose. With every detail considered.

You are God's poem.

Now think about what that means. When a poet sits down to write, they do not throw words together randomly and hope something meaningful emerges. They choose. They consider every word, every line, every pause, every breath in the rhythm of the piece. Every element of a great poem is intentional. Nothing is accidental. Even the spaces, even what is not said, is chosen.

God crafted you with that same intentionality.

The way your mind works. The way you feel things deeply. The specific combination of gifts and personality and passion that makes you different from every other human being who has ever lived or ever will live. The things that make you laugh. The things that break your heart. The problems in the world that you cannot walk past without feeling called to do something about them. All of it, all of it, was considered and chosen and crafted by a God who was making something specific on purpose.

> THE WORD: **Yatsar (yah-TSAR)**
>
> *To form, to shape, to mold — the word of a potter working clay.*
> Used in Genesis 2:7 when God formed man from the dust, and
> in Isaiah 64:8 when Isaiah cries out 'We are the clay, and You
> our potter.' This is hands-on, intimate, deliberate work. God
> did not speak you into existence at a distance. He formed you.

My Grandfather and the Music He Made

My grandfather J.L. Lowe spent his life in jazz. And the
more I have thought about what that means, the more I
understand something about how God designs people.

In jazz, the musician does not just play the notes on the
page. They interpret. They feel. They bring something to
the music that nobody else can bring because it comes
from their specific way of hearing the world. Two jazz
musicians can play the same song and it will sound
different, not because one of them is doing it wrong, but
because they are each bringing their original design to the
work.

There is a moment in great jazz when you can feel that the
musician is not just performing, they are being. They are
fully themselves in the music. And when you hear that,
you cannot mistake it for anything else.

That is what it looks like when someone is operating fully
in their God-given design.

God designed you a certain way. With a specific sound.
With a specific gift. With a specific voice that, when you
stop trying to sound like someone else and simply be
yourself, people will lean in because they have never heard
it quite like that before.

That is not arrogance. That is stewardship of what God made.

Comparison Is a Theological Problem

I want to say something bluntly, because I think it needs to be said plainly: comparison is not just unpleasant. It is a theological error.

When you compare your design to someone else's and conclude that theirs is better, you are telling God that His creative choices for your life were inferior. You are essentially saying: the poem You wrote is not as good as that one. You should have made me differently. The way You crafted me is less than.

That is not humility. That is an insult to the Craftsman.

Comparison is a failure to trust God's design choices. It is a refusal to believe that what He crafted in you is good, sufficient, and exactly what He intended.

God does not make copies. Let that settle in.

There is nobody else on this earth with your exact design. Nobody else with your specific combination of gifts, personality, experience, perspective, and calling. Nobody else who has been placed exactly where you have been placed, with access to the exact people you have access to, with the specific assignment that God wrote for your specific life.

Nobody else can be you.

Complete, Not Incomplete

> *"And you are complete in Him, who is the head of all principality and power."* — **Colossians 2:10 (NKJV)**

Complete. In Him. Right now. Not becoming complete. Not almost complete pending better performance or deeper spiritual maturity. Complete.

The value of a poem is not determined by how much editing it still needs. The value of a poem is determined by the one who wrote it. And God wrote you. Which means your value is not a moving target that you spend your life chasing. It was established at the writing.

You are not less valuable because you are still growing. You are not less significant because the story is still being written. You are not less worthy because the process is not finished.

You are complete in Him. Right now. In this season. In this body. In this life. With these gifts and these limitations and this specific story that has never existed before and will never exist again.

You are God's poem. And it is a good one.

> ***You*** *are not random.* ***You*** *are crafted. God's poiema - His poem, His masterpiece. Made with intention, on purpose, and complete in Him.*

1. What parts of your design have you been apologizing for, minimizing, or treating as a liability? Write them down. Then ask: what if God placed those there on purpose?

2. Where have you been comparing your design to someone else's and concluding that yours is less? How has that comparison been costing you?

3. What does it mean to you personally that God calls you His poem — His poiema — crafted with intentionality and purpose?

"I will praise You, for I am fearfully and wonderfully made; marvelous are Your works, and that my soul knows very well."

— **Psalm 139:14 (NKJV)**

PRAY THIS

Father,

I receive this today with open hands. I receive the truth that I am Your workmanship — Your poiema — crafted with intention, with skill, with a specific design that was chosen before I ever took my first breath.Forgive me for the times I minimized what You made. For the times I looked at someone else's design and wished I had been made differently. For agreeing with the world's verdict that I was not enough rather than standing on Your declaration that I am complete in Christ.Today I choose to stop letting comparison steal my joy in what You gave me. I choose to honor Your craftsmanship by taking it seriously.I am Yours. You made me well. I believe that today.In Jesus' name, Amen.

PART THREE

THE LABELS THE WORLD TRIES TO GIVE YOU

"Anything that defines you apart from God will eventually exhaust you."

CHAPTER 5

The Achievement Label

What happens when what you do becomes who you are

> *If you stopped doing everything you do for God tomorrow — would you still know who you are to God?*

Sit with that question before you answer it. Because the knee-jerk response for most people who have been in church for any length of time is: of course. Of course my identity is not in what I do. Of course I know my worth comes from God and not from my output.

And then Monday morning comes. And the project does not land the way you hoped. Or the ministry feels dry. Or the numbers are not moving. Or someone else got the recognition for the work you put in. And something shifts inside you that tells the truth about where your identity was actually parked.

We say identity is in Christ. We live like identity is in the results.

This chapter is about the gap between those two things, and why closing that gap might be the most important work you do this year.

The Achievement Trap Is Everywhere

Let me be honest about something. The achievement trap is not just a worldly problem. It is not just about career ambition or social climbing or keeping up with what you see online. The achievement trap lives inside the church just as comfortably as it lives anywhere else. Maybe more comfortably, because in church we have found a way to dress it up in the language of calling and purpose and fruitfulness until it is nearly unrecognizable.

We call it stewardship when we grind ourselves down to nothing trying to produce results for God. We call it faithfulness when we pile on more and more service until there is no margin left and our families barely know us. We call it humility when we quietly measure every sermon, every ministry moment, every offering, every outreach against what someone else is producing, and feel the familiar sting when ours comes up shorter.

But it is not stewardship. It is not faithfulness. It is not humility. It is identity built on a foundation that cannot hold.

Achievement-based identity is seductive because it works, until it doesn't. When you are winning, when you are producing, when the numbers are good and the recognition is coming and things are moving the way you planned, you feel significant. You feel certain. You feel like you know who you are.

But then the season changes.

And if your identity is built on achievement, a bad season does not just affect your circumstances. It attacks your sense of self.

The Martha Moment

"Martha, Martha, you are worried and troubled about many things. But one thing is needed, and Mary has chosen that good part, which will not be taken away from her." — Luke 10:41-42 (NKJV)

I want to be careful here, because this passage is often used to suggest that serving is less important than sitting and listening, and that is not the point. Martha's service was real and it mattered. The meal needed to be made. Hospitality was not trivial.

The point is not that she was working. The point is what the work had become for her.

Notice the words Jesus uses: worried and troubled about many things. That is not the language of someone who is simply busy. That is the language of someone whose emotional state is entirely tied to the outcome of their output. Martha was not just cooking a meal. Martha was managing her worth through the meal.

That is what achievement-based identity does. It ties your inner state to your outer output. And because output is always subject to circumstances you cannot fully control, your inner state is never stable for long.

Jesus was not criticizing her service. He was naming her condition. You have allowed what you are doing to become more real to you than who you are. Come back to the one thing.

The Difference Between Expression and Earning

There is a version of achievement that flows from a settled identity. It looks like this: I know who I am in God. I know I am chosen, designed, called, placed. And from that settled place, I work. I serve. I create. I lead. I build. Not to prove something. Not to maintain a sense of worth. But because the gifts and the calling and the design that God placed in me are naturally expressing themselves through what I do.

That version of achievement is energizing. It is sustainable. It produces good fruit without grinding you into the ground, because it is not carrying a weight it was never designed to carry.

Then there is the version of achievement that IS the identity. It looks like this: I need to produce, serve, lead, and perform at a certain level in order to feel like I matter. My worth is measured by my output. When I am not producing, I feel invisible. When I am producing, I feel significant.

That version of achievement is exhausting. It is unsustainable. It will eventually collapse under the weight of what it is trying to carry, because no amount of human

output can sustain a human soul. Only God can do that.
The question is not whether you should work hard. The
question is where the work is coming from.

Is your work an expression of who you are? Or is it an
attempt to establish who you are?

One is freedom. The other is bondage that has learned to
look like faithfulness.

THE WORD: **Shabbat (shah-BAHT)**

*Rest, cessation, to stop — the sacred practice God built into
creation itself.*

God did not rest on the seventh day because He was tired. He
rested to establish a pattern. Identity is not built through
constant production. It is sustained through rhythms of rest
that remind you that your worth does not depend on your
output. Shabbat is a weekly declaration: I am more than what
I make.

*"Come to Me, all you who labor and are heavy laden,
and I will give you rest. Take My yoke upon you and
learn from Me, for I am gentle and lowly in heart,
and you will find rest for your souls. For My yoke is
easy and My burden is light."* — Matthew 11:28-30
(NKJV)

If ministry feels heavy, check whether you are carrying
God's assignment or your own identity management.
Because God's yoke is described as easy and His burden as
light. That does not mean easy as in effortless. It means
easy as in fitted correctly.

If what you are carrying is crushing you, something is off.

*Achievement is a gift. But when it becomes the foundation of **your** identity rather than an expression of it, a bad season doesn't just change **your** circumstances. It attacks **your** sense of self.*

GOING DEEPER

Take your time with these. Write honestly. This is your book.

1. Where does your sense of worth fluctuate based on results? Be specific — what seasons, roles, or metrics have you tied your identity to?

2. What would you tell yourself if every achievement-based title you currently hold was removed tomorrow? Write the honest answer, not the spiritual one.

3. Is your work an expression of who you are in God, or an attempt to establish who you are? Where is the line for you right now?

A WORD TO CARRY

"I have been crucified with Christ; it is no longer I who live, but Christ lives in me; and the life which I now live in the flesh I live by faith in the Son of God."

— **Galatians 2:20 (NKJV)**

Father,

I confess that I have built more of my identity on what I produce than I have wanted to admit. I have called it faithfulness when it was actually fear, fear that if I stop performing, I stop mattering.Forgive me for making Your yoke heavy by carrying things You never asked me to carry. Forgive me for measuring my worth by my output instead of by what You declared over me before I ever did anything.Teach me the rhythm of rest. Teach me what it feels like to work from a settled place rather than a striving one. Let my service be an expression of identity, not a search for it.I am more than what I make. Help me live like I believe that.In Jesus' name, Amen.

CHAPTER 6

The Pain Label

Your worst season is not your definition

> **Is it possible that you have built your house on what happened to you — and if the building fell, you would not know who you were in the rubble?**

This is the chapter I want to handle with the most care. Because pain labels are the stickiest ones we carry. They have the most emotional history behind them. They are often the most justified, you did go through that, it was real, it was hard, it shaped you. And I am not here to minimize any of it.

But I want to make a distinction today that I believe, if you let it settle, will do more for your freedom than almost anything else in this book.

There is a difference between pain that has been part of your story and pain that has become your identity.

One is honest. The other is a trap.

When the Wound Becomes the Name

Think about the people you know who have been through something hard. A loss. A betrayal. A trauma. A prolonged season of suffering.

Now think about how some of those people talk about themselves years later. Not about what they went through, but about who they are. The woman who lost her baby and fifteen years later still introduces herself primarily through that loss. The man who was betrayed in ministry and whose entire framework for relationships is still being run through that one wound.

The pain is real. The wound was real. But something happened along the way that turned a thing that happened to them into a thing that became them.

And that is the pain label. It is when what you experienced becomes what you answer to.

Sugah, what happened to you is part of your story. It is not the title of your story. There is a difference, and it matters more than I can fully express in one chapter.

THE WORD: **Ra'ah (rah-AH)**

Evil, harm, trouble, distress — the hard and painful things of this world.

Genesis 50:20 — Joseph says to his brothers: 'You intended to harm me (ra'ah), but God intended it for good.' The same event seen from two entirely different vantage points. What the enemy meant to use to define and destroy you, God has been using to prepare and position you.

The Joseph Principle

> *"But as for you, you meant evil against me; but God meant it for good, in order to bring it about as it is this day, to save many people alive."* — **Genesis 50:20 (NKJV)**

Joseph did not say: what happened to me was not that bad. He looked at all of it clearly and named it honestly, you meant evil against me. He was not performing forgiveness he had not processed.

But he had arrived at something that many people never reach: the understanding that what happened to him was not the final word on who he was or what his life meant. God had been in it all along. Not causing the cruelty, but present in it. Working through it. Positioning him through the very suffering that was meant to destroy him.

That is not a theology that minimizes pain. That is a theology that refuses to give pain the last word.

Your pain has a purpose. But it is not your identity.

THE WORD: **Shavar (shah-VAR)**

To break, to shatter — but also the word used when God heals and restores the brokenhearted.

Isaiah 61:1 says God was sent to heal the brokenhearted — and the word for brokenhearted uses this same root. God does not avoid the shattered places. He moves toward them. He does not throw out what is broken. He heals it.

Isaiah 61 and the Exchange

> *"He has sent Me to heal the brokenhearted, to proclaim liberty to the captives... to give them beauty for ashes, the oil of joy for mourning, the garment of praise for the spirit of heaviness."* — Isaiah 61:1-3 (NKJV)

I want you to look at the exchange God is offering.

Beauty for ashes. Oil of joy for mourning. A garment of praise for a spirit of heaviness.

In each case, something is given in place of something else. But here is what I want you to notice: the exchange requires you to bring what you have. You cannot receive beauty while you are clutching the ashes. You cannot receive the oil of joy if you refuse to release the mourning.

You cannot put on the garment of praise if you are unwilling to take off the spirit of heaviness.

The exchange is real. But it is an exchange. God is not asking you to pretend the ashes are not there. He is asking you to bring what you have, the honest, real, unfiltered truth of what you have been through, and trust Him to exchange it for something better.

But you have to open your hands.

Some of us have been holding the ashes so long that we have forgotten we have a choice about whether to keep them.

But ashes are not your inheritance. Beauty is.

Mourning is not your permanent address. Joy is available.

The spirit of heaviness is not who you are. The garment of praise is already prepared.

You have to be willing to make the exchange.

***Your** pain has a purpose. But it is not **your** identity. The wound is not **your** name. What God is building from **your** hardest seasons is greater than what the enemy tried to make them mean.*

Take your time with these. Write honestly. This is your book.

1. What pain label have you been carrying? Name it specifically. When did it stop being something that happened to you and start being who you are?

2. Isaiah 61 describes an exchange, beauty for ashes, joy for mourning. What would you need to release to receive that exchange? Be honest about what you have been holding onto.

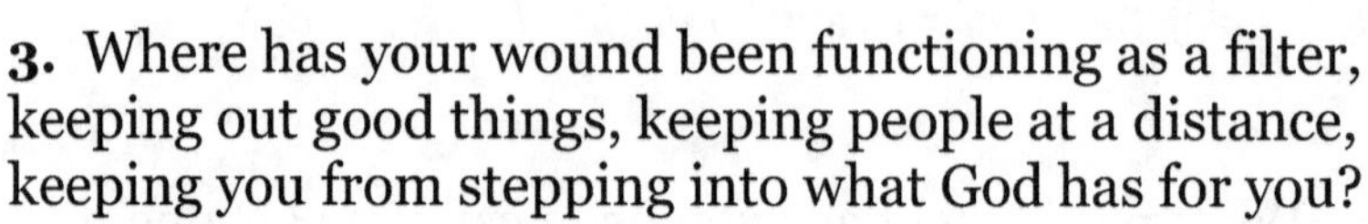

3. Where has your wound been functioning as a filter, keeping out good things, keeping people at a distance, keeping you from stepping into what God has for you?

Write a letter to your wound. Acknowledge what it cost you. Then tell it that it is no longer your name.

"And we know that all things work together for good to those who love God, to those who are the called according to His purpose."

— **Romans 8:28 (NKJV)**

Let's Pray

Father,

I bring You the honest truth today. I have been holding ashes longer than I needed to. I have let what happened to me become how I define myself, and I have called that survival when some of it was just hiding.I do not want to minimize what I went through. It was real. It hurt. It shaped me in ways I am still discovering.But today I am choosing to believe that it is not my name. That You have not wasted one moment of it. That what the enemy meant for evil, You have been working for good, even in the parts I still do not understand. I open my hands. I bring You the ashes. I am ready for the exchange.Heal what I have been carrying. Build something new from what I thought was only rubble. Show me who I am outside of what happened to me.In Jesus' name, Amen.

CHAPTER 7

The Approval Label

Your worth cannot be measured by applause

> **Can you do what God has called you to do even when nobody is clapping?**

That question is not rhetorical. I want you to actually sit with it. Because the honest answer, not the answer you would give in a Sunday school class but the answer that shows up in how you actually live, will tell you more about where your identity is parked than almost anything else.

The approval trap is one of the most common identity problems I encounter. And I want to be careful in this chapter about how I handle it, because it is also one of the most misunderstood. People hear "you are seeking approval" and they feel accused of something shameful, when really what they are dealing with is a deeply human need that has simply been placed in the wrong hands.

So let's start with some grace before we get to the truth.

The Need Is Not the Problem

God designed human beings for community. He designed us to be known, to be seen, to be in relationship with people who speak truth over us, celebrate our growth, and remind us of who we are on the days we forget. That need is not a flaw. It is a feature.

So needing encouragement from people is not weakness. Wanting to be affirmed and celebrated by the people in your life is not vanity. Being genuinely moved when someone sees your gifts and names them, that is healthy. That is community working the way God intended.

Here is where the problem starts. The problem is not the need. The problem is when you cannot function without it.

The problem is when the presence or absence of someone else's approval becomes the gauge by which you measure your own worth. When a lack of response to something you shared sends you spiraling. When silence from someone who matters to you undoes every true thing you have ever believed about yourself.

That is when affirmation becomes addiction. And that addiction will quietly and steadily steal your life, your calling, and your obedience.

The Difference Between Affirmation and Approval

Affirmation is when someone speaks truth over you. They see what God put in you and they name it. They celebrate your growth. They encourage you when doubt is loud. Affirmation is a gift you receive from people who love you well, and it is one of the most beautiful functions of genuine community.

Approval is different in one critical way: you need it in order to feel okay.

Affirmation says: I love when people see and celebrate what God is doing in me.

Approval says: I need people to see and celebrate me or I do not know if what God is doing in me is real.

One is a gift you receive gratefully. The other is a drug you cannot live without.

> THE WORD: **Kavod (kah-VODE)**
> *Glory, weight, honor — but literally, heaviness or substance.*
> The word kavod is used for both human honor and divine glory. But notice the root: weight. Real significance has substance. It is not dependent on being seen. It does not evaporate when the room stops watching. Kavod that comes from God has a weight that human applause can never provide and human silence can never remove.

What the Approval Trap Actually Costs You

Your approval addiction does not just affect you. It affects every person God intended to reach through your authentic, uncompromised, Spirit-led self.

When you shrink your calling to fit the size of someone else's comfort, you are not being humble. You are being disobedient. When you silence the voice God gave you because you are calculating how it will be received, you are not being wise. You are being controlled by the wrong thing. And every person who needed the real word gets a diluted version instead.

> *"For do I now persuade men, or God? Or do I seek to please men? For if I still pleased men, I would not be a bondservant of Christ."* — Galatians 1:10 (NKJV)

Paul makes this stark. Pleasing men and serving Christ are not always compatible. There will be moments, and they will come, guaranteed, when what God is asking you to do will cost you approval. When the obedient move is the unpopular one. When the word that needs to be said is the one nobody wants to hear.

To delight in, to take pleasure in, to desire — what God genuinely wants.

Psalm 149:4 says the Lord takes delight (chaphets) in His people. This is not reluctant tolerance. This is genuine pleasure. God's approval of you is not the cold, transactional validation you receive from a like count. It is the warm, personal, covenant delight of a Father in a child He chose.

The Wall Was Not Strength

There was a season in my life when the approval trap had me in a way I did not fully recognize at the time. And my response to needing approval, the defense mechanism I built, was not to people-please. It was the opposite. I built walls. I became sharp. I became difficult to get close to. I was the kind of person who would cut you with a look and call it confidence.

And here is what I want you to hear: both responses, the people-pleasing and the armor-building ,come from the same root. They are both responses to the fear of being rejected. One tries to earn the approval. The other tries to make the approval irrelevant by refusing to need it.

But you cannot make approval irrelevant by building walls. You can only make it irrelevant by finding something more solid to stand on.

What God showed me in that season is that the wall was not strength. Strength does not need a wall. Strength can be open and vulnerable and still stand firm because it is rooted in something that cannot be shaken. The wall was evidence of weakness, specifically, the weakness of an identity that had not yet been secured in Christ.

Your *worth cannot be measured by applause.*
*God's opinion of **you** is the only one that contains*
the full picture — and it has not changed.

GOING DEEPER

Take your time with these. Write honestly. This is your book.

1. Be honest: Can you do what God is calling you to do right now even if nobody acknowledges it? Where specifically does the need for approval make you hesitate or hold back?

2. What is the difference in your life between affirmation (a gift) and approval (a need)? Where have you crossed that line?

3. Think about the last time you softened, delayed, or silenced something God was asking you to do because you were afraid of how it would be received. Write what happened and what it cost.

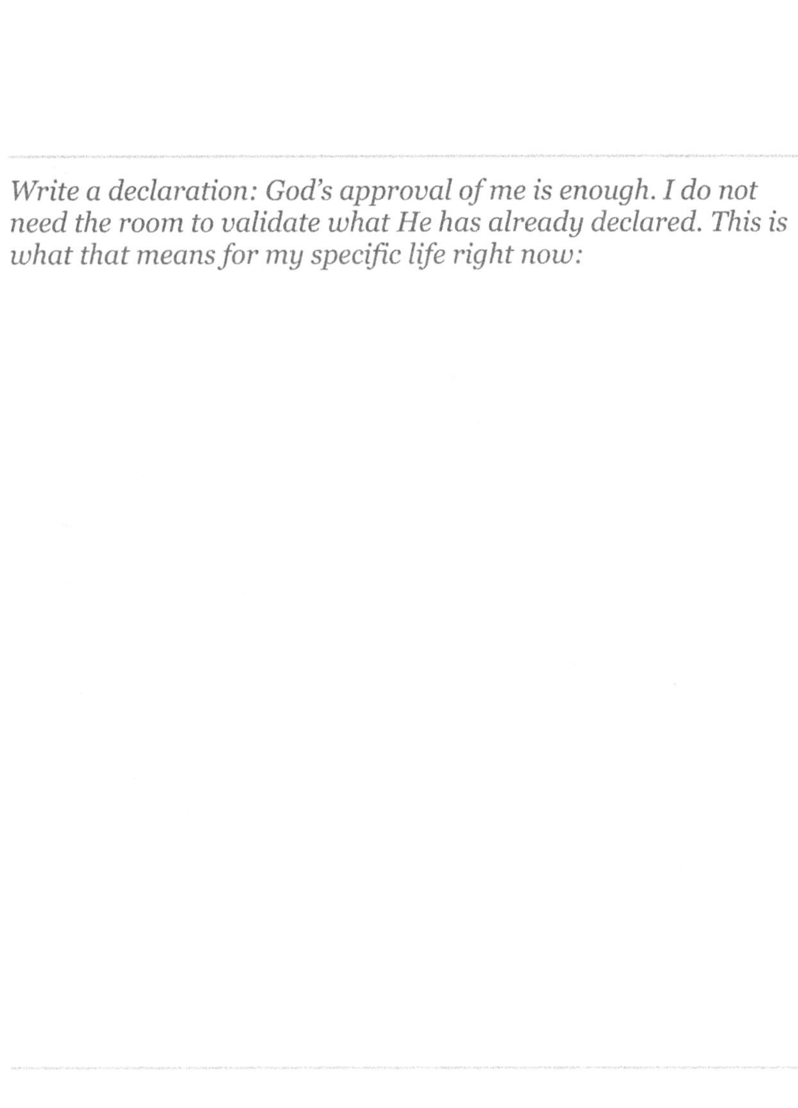

Write a declaration: God's approval of me is enough. I do not need the room to validate what He has already declared. This is what that means for my specific life right now:

"For they loved the praise of men more than the praise of God."

— **John 12:43 (NKJV)**

Let's Pray..

Father,

I confess that I have given other people's opinions too much power over my life. I have let the presence or absence of applause tell me whether I was enough. I have shaped and managed and performed versions of myself trying to earn what You already freely gave me before I ever did anything to deserve it.Forgive me for the times I softened what You told me to say because I was afraid of the response. Forgive me for building walls when You were trying to build relationship. Forgive me for mistaking armor for strength.Today I choose Your opinion over every other voice. I choose to be faithful in the private places where nobody is watching. I choose to stop performing and start being, because who You made me to be is more than enough.Your approval is my foundation. And it is enough.In Jesus' name, Amen.

CHAPTER 8

The Role Label

When the title becomes the person — and then the title leaves

---

> *If every role you currently play was stripped away tomorrow — parent, spouse, minister, professional, leader — who would be left?*

Take a moment with that. Really take a moment.

Because I have found that most people, when they are honest, have a harder time answering that question than they expected. We can usually describe ourselves through our roles without much effort. I am a mother. I am a pastor. I am a business owner. I am a wife. I am a leader in my community. Those answers come quickly.

But strip the roles and ask again, who are you? ....and the room gets quiet.

That silence is not a sign of failure. It is a diagnosis. It means somewhere along the way, the role became the identity. And the role, as important and real as it is, was never designed to carry that weight.

Jacob at the Jabbok

There is a story in Genesis 32 that I want to spend some time with, because I believe it is one of the richest pictures in all of Scripture of what it looks like when God confronts an identity built on the wrong foundation.

Jacob. The name itself is the whole story. In Hebrew, the name Jacob — Ya'aqov — comes from the word for heel, and it carried the connotation of supplanting, grasping, even deceiving. Jacob was the man who grabbed his twin brother's heel in the womb. The man who purchased Esau's birthright for a bowl of stew. The man who deceived his aging father to steal the blessing meant for his brother. He got through life by being clever, by maneuvering, by making things happen through his own strategy rather than through trust in God.

His name was his identity. And his identity was a problem.

> *"So He said to him, 'What is your name?' He said, 'Jacob."* — **Genesis 32:27 (NKJV)**

God already knew his name. He did not need the information. But Jacob needed to say it.

Say it out loud. Say what you have been. Stop managing the image. Stop performing the more acceptable version. Just say it plain: this is who I have been. This is the name I have been answering to.

Before God could give Jacob the new name, Jacob had to acknowledge the old one.

THE WORD: **Ya'aqov (yah-ah-KOV)**

Jacob — from the root meaning heel, to supplant, to grasp, to deceive.

This was not just a name. It was an identity label that Jacob had been living under and living out. When God asked 'What is your name?' He was not gathering information. He was inviting confession. You cannot receive a new name while you are still pretending to be fine with the old one.

The Limp That Stayed

> *"Just as he crossed over Penuel the sun rose on him, and he limped on his hip."* — **Genesis 32:31 (NKJV)**

He walked differently for the rest of his life.

That limp was not a punishment. That limp was a permanent reminder of the encounter. Every step Jacob took from that moment forward declared: I have met God and I have been changed. I am not the same person who walked into this night.

When God changes your identity, it changes how you move through the world. Sometimes the evidence of a real encounter with God is not that everything is suddenly easy and beautiful and polished. Sometimes the evidence is that you carry a limp, a reminder of the place where you finally stopped wrestling on your own terms and surrendered to the One who was stronger.

The scars from your wrestling are not failures. They are testimony.

Do not be ashamed of your limp. It is proof of encounter.

Roles as Expression, Not Source

Roles are meant to be expressions of identity, not replacements for it.

When you know who you are in God, when that is settled, rooted, not dependent on any title or function, then your roles become the natural overflow of that. You parent from a settled place. You lead from a settled place. You serve from a settled place. You build from a settled place.

And when the role changes, as roles always eventually do, the foundation does not shake. Because the foundation was never in the role.

You were not made to be your title. You were made to bear the image of God and carry His presence into every space He places you, in every role, through every season, whether the title is impressive or invisible.

> *The role is the assignment. **You** are the person.*
> *And **you** were always more than the assignment.*

Take your time with these. Write honestly. This is your book.

1. Which role in your life has been carrying the most identity weight? What happens inside you when that role is questioned, threatened, or unavailable?

2. God asked Jacob: What is your name? He is asking you the same question right now. What name — what role, what label, what version of yourself — have you been answering to that you need to say out loud and surrender?

3. Is there a role in your life that has ended or is transitioning? Write honestly about what that has felt like, and then write what you know to be true about your identity that the role change cannot touch.

Write your honest answer: Who am I when every role is removed? Start with what you know God says, not what you feel.

"Now, therefore, you are no longer strangers and foreigners, but fellow citizens with the saints and members of the household of God."

— **Ephesians 2:19 (NKJV)**

Whew... Let's Pray..

Father,

I come to You the way Jacob came, alone, honest, and willing to say out loud what I have been answering to. I have built more of my identity on what I do and the roles I fill than I have wanted to admit. I have called those roles my calling when sometimes they were actually my cover, a way to feel significant without having to settle the deeper question of who I am to You. Forgive me for letting the title carry more than it was designed to carry. Forgive me for confusing the assignment with the person. Today I release the roles back to You as expressions of identity, not the source of it. Whether my roles shift, grow, change, or end, I am still Your child. I am still chosen, known, crafted, and loved. Tell me my new name, Lord. I am ready to hear it. In Jesus' name, Amen.

PART FOUR

LIVING FROM THE LABEL GOD WROTE

"Before anyone else had a pen, God had already written the truest thing about you."

CHAPTER 9

Known, Not Overlooked

Being unseen by people does not mean unseen by God

> *Have you ever shown up faithfully, done everything right, poured out everything you had — and still felt completely invisible?*

Not the obvious rejection kind of invisible, where someone actively excludes you or speaks against you. That pain is real, but at least it has a name. At least you can point to it.

I am talking about the other kind. The quiet kind. The kind that comes from being present but not truly seen. From doing good work that nobody acknowledges. From carrying gifts that nobody seems to recognize. From showing up with everything you have to offer, again and again, and watching the recognition go somewhere else.

The pain of invisibility is one of the loneliest pains there is. Because it does not announce itself. It accumulates. Day after day, season after season, it just quietly piles up. And somewhere in that accumulation, a lie starts to form.

The lie says: if no one sees you, maybe you do not matter.

This chapter is about that lie. And about the truth that is stronger than it.

What Psalm 139 Actually Says

> *"O Lord, You have searched me and known me. You know my sitting down and my rising up; You understand my thought afar off. You comprehend my path and my lying down, and are acquainted with all my ways. For there is not a word on my tongue, but behold, O Lord, You know it altogether."* — **Psalm 139:1-4 (NKJV)**

Every phrase in these four verses is intentional.

You have searched me. The Hebrew behind that word is not casual awareness. It is active investigation, the kind of searching that goes into every room, opens every drawer, does not skip the dark corners or the locked doors. God has not glanced at you. He has searched you.

You know my sitting down and my rising up. The ordinary moments. The Monday morning before anyone else is awake. The Wednesday afternoon when nothing significant is happening. The moments that will never make anyone's highlight reel. God is present in those.

For there is not a word on my tongue but You know it altogether. Every word you have ever said in an empty room. Every prayer you have prayed that felt like it went nowhere. He has heard every word.

THE WORD: **Yada (yah-DAH)**

To know intimately — not surface knowledge but deep, thorough, personal acquaintance.

God does not know about you the way you know about a public figure. He knows you the way you know someone you have lived with, learned with, been present with through every season. His yada of you is complete. Nothing is missing from the picture He has of who you are.

El Roi — The God Who Sees

> *"She called the name of the Lord who spoke to her, You-Are-the-God-Who-Sees; for she said, "Have I also here seen Him who sees me?"* — Genesis 16:13 (NKJV)

El Roi. The God who sees.

That is not a minor title. That is not a footnote in her story. It is the whole revelation of the moment. Hagar, dismissed by people, invisible in the narrative, sent away from the household that should have protected her, discovered something in the wilderness that would anchor her for the rest of her life.

God sees what people miss.

He sees you in the seasons when the recognition goes elsewhere. He sees the faithfulness that never made it into anyone's testimony. He sees the prayers you prayed in the middle of the night that nobody witnessed. He sees the work you did that someone else got credit for. He sees the courage it took to show up again after the last time you were passed over.

He sees all of it. And He does not forget what He sees.

THE WORD: **El Roi (el ROH-ee)**
The God Who Sees — the name Hagar gave God in Genesis 16.
This is the only place in Scripture where a human being gives God a name. And the name came not from a mountaintop revelation or a moment of triumph. It came from a wilderness encounter when Hagar had been dismissed and forgotten by everyone around her. Your unseen seasons are exactly where El Roi shows up.

The Hidden Season Has a Purpose

The size of your public impact is often proportional to the depth of your private formation.

Think about Moses. Forty years in the wilderness before he stood before Pharaoh. Forty years of obscurity, of tending someone else's flock, of being far from the palace and the power and the platform he had once occupied. Forty years of hiddenness that were forming in him the character, the humility, and the intimacy with God that the assignment of leading a nation would require.

Think about Joseph. Years in prison before the palace. Years of being forgotten by the people he helped. And in those years, not in spite of them but through them, God was building something that the throne room would require.

None of these were delays. All of them were designs.

Your hidden season is not evidence that God overlooked you. It is evidence that He trusts you with the formation that most people cannot endure.

> *"...that your charitable deed may be in secret; and your Father who sees in secret will Himself reward you openly."* — Matthew 6:4 (NKJV)

Every quiet act of obedience when nobody was watching, God saw it. Every seed you planted in ground that has not broken open yet, God saw it. Every prayer you prayed in the dark when you were not sure anyone was listening, God heard every word.

None of it was wasted. None of it was unseen. None of it has been forgotten by the only One whose opinion will outlast this season.

Being unseen by people does not mean unseen by God. El Roi sees every act of hidden faithfulness. Not one moment has been missed. Not one seed forgotten.

GOING DEEPER

Take your time with these. Write honestly. This is your book.

1. Describe a season when you felt genuinely invisible — when you were faithful and nobody seemed to notice. How did that invisibility shape what you believed about your worth?

2. God sees in secret. What is something you have done faithfully in private — something nobody acknowledged — that you need to surrender to God as an act of trust in His seeing?

3. Is there a hidden season in your life right now? What might God be forming in you in this quiet place that could not be built in public?

Write an honest response to El Roi — the God who sees. Tell Him about the unseen faithfulness you have been carrying. Then receive His response.

A WORD TO CARRY

"Your eyes saw my substance, being yet unformed. And in Your book they all were written, the days fashioned for me, when as yet there were none of them."

— Psalm 139:16 (NKJV)

Father,

I come to You from a place of honesty today. There are seasons when being unseen by people has started to feel like being unseen by You. When the silence of the hidden place started feeling like abandonment instead of preparation. And today I bring all of that to You.Thank You for seeing me. Not the managed version. Not the performed version. The real me, the one who is sometimes tired, sometimes overlooked, sometimes aching to be recognized. You know that person. You love that person. You see every act of faithfulness I have ever poured out in secret.Help me trust the hidden season. Help me stay faithful when faithfulness is not being rewarded with visibility. Help me let Your seeing be enough.I receive Your gaze today. And I declare that it is enough.In Jesus' name, Amen.

CHAPTER 10

Accepted, Not Tolerated

You are not on probation with God

> *Do you approach God like a guest, grateful to be there, careful not to overstay, braced for the moment when you finally do something that costs you your place?*

Be honest. Not the theological answer. The lived one.

Because there is a version of faith that looks like devotion from the outside but is actually running on fear underneath. It shows up in how people pray, carefully, cautiously, as if the wrong words might change the outcome. It shows up in how people serve, compulsively, never stopping, because stopping might mean the goodwill runs out. It shows up in how people approach God after they have stumbled, at a distance, waiting until they feel cleaned up enough to come close.

And it all comes from the same root: a deep, often unexamined belief that the welcome is conditional. That the acceptance is provisional, good as long as you perform well, subject to review whenever you do not.

I want to dismantle that belief in this chapter. Not gently, because gentle is not what it needs. It needs to be named for what it is and replaced with what is actually true.

You are not on probation with God. You are not a guest in His house. You are not tolerated. You are accepted. And the difference between those two things changes everything about how you live.

> *"...to the praise of the glory of His grace, by which He made us accepted in the Beloved."* — Ephesians 1:6 (NKJV)

Notice the language. He made us accepted. Not: He evaluates us periodically and finds us acceptable when we behave. Not: He reviews our performance and extends provisional acceptance. He made us accepted. Past tense. Done. Settled.

And this acceptance did not come from your track record. It came from His grace. The making happened in Christ, through Christ, because of Christ. And nothing you do can add to it or subtract from it because you did not produce it in the first place.

> THE WORD: **Ratsah (rah-TSAH)**
> *To be pleased with, to accept favorably, to take delight in.*
> Psalm 149:4 says the Lord takes delight — ratsah — in His people. This is not the cold, reluctant tolerance of someone putting up with you. This is warm, genuine pleasure. The same word used when God looked at His creation and called it good. He does not merely accept you. He delights in you.

The Guest vs. The Family

Think about being a guest in someone's home. You ask where to sit rather than just sitting anywhere. You watch the clock, conscious of not overstaying your welcome. You present your best behavior because the welcome could be withdrawn.

Now think about being family in that same home. Family does not ask where to sit, they know where the plates are.

Family does not watch the clock because there is no clock to watch. Family can be themselves, tired, uncertain, messy, real, without worrying that being genuinely themselves will cost them their place.

Family can disagree. Family can struggle. Family can have a terrible week and show up the following Sunday like they live there, because they do.

> *"Now, therefore, you are no longer strangers and foreigners, but fellow citizens with the saints and members of the household of God."* — **Ephesians 2:19 (NKJV)**

God did not just save you. He brought you in. And brought in means you do not have to keep earning the right to be there. The right was settled when you were brought in.

The Prodigal's Return

> *"And he arose and came to his father. But when he was still a great way off, his father saw him and had compassion, and ran and fell on his neck and kissed him."* — Luke 15:20 (NKJV)

Still a great way off.

The father did not wait for the son to arrive at the house, deliver the prepared speech, and demonstrate adequate remorse. He saw him coming when he was still a great distance away, which tells us the father had been watching. Looking. Waiting for the moment when the son who had left might be coming back.

And he ran.

Fathers in that culture did not run. It was beneath the dignity of a patriarch to hike up his robes and sprint down the road. But this father ran because the running was more important than the dignity.

He fell on his neck and kissed him before the son could deliver his speech. Before the apology was complete. Before the negotiation could begin.

The father's acceptance was not conditional on the quality of the son's repentance. It was simply waiting for the son to turn around and come home.

That is your Father. That is how He receives you.

Stop rehearsing the speech. Just turn around and come home.

THE WORD: **Racham (rah-KHAM)**

Deep compassion, tender mercy — from the root word for womb.

This is the word behind the Old Testament concept of God's mercy — a mercy so intimate it is described with the image of a mother's love for the child she carried. God's acceptance of you is not the cold tolerance of a distant judge. It carries the warmth of racham — a love that is tender, personal, and rooted in the deepest kind of knowing.

> *"There is therefore now no condemnation to those who are in Christ Jesus, who do not walk according to the flesh, but according to the Spirit."* — **Romans 8:1 (NKJV)**

No condemnation. Not reduced condemnation. Not condemnation held in reserve for the next major failure. No condemnation.

That word, no, is doing more work in that sentence than we usually let it do.

You are not tolerated. You are accepted. Not provisionally. Not conditionally. In Christ, by grace, made accepted — permanently and completely.

Take your time with these. Write honestly. This is your book.

1. Be honest: In what specific ways do you approach God like a guest rather than a family member? What does that look like practically in your prayer life, your service, your response when you fail?

2. Where have you been confusing conviction with condemnation? Write about a specific time the enemy used a stumble to convince you that distance from God was the appropriate response.

3. The father ran before the son finished his speech. What speech have you been rehearsing — what do you think you need to get right before God will fully receive you? Write it out, and then write Romans 8:1 over it.

A WORD TO CARRY

"Let us therefore come boldly to the throne of grace, that we may obtain mercy and find grace to help in time of need."

— **Hebrews 4:16 (NKJV)**

Father,

I have been approaching You like a guest, grateful, but careful. Present, but not quite settled. Serving, but always with one eye on whether my welcome is holding. And today I want to lay that down. Your Word says You made me accepted in the Beloved. Not conditionally. Not provisionally. Made accepted. I receive that today, not as a nice idea but as the foundation I stand on. Forgive me for every time I hid from You after I stumbled, as if the hiding was more appropriate than the running. Forgive me for treating Your house like a place I have to earn rather than a place I belong. I come home today. Not with a rehearsed speech. Just as I am.Thank You for running toward me.In Jesus' name, Amen.

CHAPTER 11

Sealed, Not Temporary

What God marked, the enemy cannot erase

> **Have you been living like your relationship with God is one bad week away from being revoked?**

Like your standing with Him is fragile. Like you are walking a tightrope and the wrong step will send everything crashing. Like the faith you carry is held together with something temporary, and under enough pressure, it will give way.

If that is where you have been living, I want to introduce you to a word that is about to change the ground you stand on.

Sealed.

Not labeled. Not tagged. Not conditionally approved pending future performance. Sealed.

That one word, when it fully lands in your spirit, will do more for your stability than any amount of spiritual effort. Because sealed means the question of your standing is not open for renegotiation.

The Difference Between a Label and a Seal

A label is applied on the surface. It tells you what something is called or what value was assigned to it. But a label is temporary by nature. It can be removed, replaced, or overwritten.

A seal is different in every meaningful way. In the ancient world, a seal was not applied lightly. When a king pressed his signet ring into wax, he was doing something with weight and consequence behind it. That seal meant three things without ambiguity: this belongs to the king. This carries his authority. And this cannot be tampered with without consequence.

> *"In Him you also trusted, after you heard the word of truth, the gospel of your salvation; in whom also, having believed, you were sealed with the Holy Spirit of promise."* — **Ephesians 1:13 (NKJV)**

You were sealed. Past tense. Completed action. Not in process. Not partially sealed pending further evaluation. Sealed. And notice the sequence: you heard, you believed, you were sealed. Not you heard, you believed, you behaved well for a sustained period, you were sealed. The sealing followed the believing. It did not follow the proving.

THE WORD: **Chatham (khah-THAM)**

To seal, to close up, to mark with a signet — declaring ownership and authority.

Song of Solomon 8:6 says: 'Set me as a seal upon your heart.' The seal is intimate. It is not placed from a distance on something of mild interest. God sealed you close, on His heart, as a declaration of permanent ownership and covenant love. The seal means: this one is Mine.

Nothing Can Separate

> *"For I am persuaded that neither death nor life, nor angels nor principalities nor powers, nor things present nor things to come, nor height nor depth, nor any other created thing, shall be able to separate us from the love of God which is in Christ Jesus our Lord."* — **Romans 8:38-39 (NKJV)**

Look at what Paul does here. He goes category by category, life, death, angels, powers, present things, future things, height, depth, and he eliminates each one as a possible separation between you and the love of God. He is so thorough that he closes with "nor any other created thing" just in case something was missed.

Nothing. Not a single thing in all of creation can separate you from the love of God in Christ.

Now here is the question that follows from that. If nothing in all of creation can separate you from God's love, why are you living like it can?

THE WORD: **Eved (EH-ved)**

Servant — but in the covenant sense, one who belongs, one who is bonded.

The biblical 'eved was not a hired hand who could walk away or be dismissed at will. Belonging was the nature of the relationship. When God calls you His servant in the covenant sense, He is not describing a job. He is describing a bond. You belong to Him. That belonging is sealed.

The Enemy's Strategy Against the Sealed

If the seal cannot be broken, why do so many believers live as though it has been?

Because the enemy is not trying to break the seal. He cannot. What he is trying to do is convince you that the seal was never there.

If he can convince you that your standing is fragile, you will live fragile. If he can make you believe that the last time you fell cost you your place, you will live at a distance from God that you do not need to live at.

The answer to accusation is not self-defense. It is declaration. Not "I have been good enough," that is the wrong argument. But: "The Lord has sealed me by His Spirit. My standing is not based on my performance. I am His and the seal does not break."

Declare your seal. Not as performance, not as spiritual showboating. As a settled, confident acknowledgment of what God has done.

I am sealed. Nothing in creation can separate me from God's love. My standing is not up for renegotiation. I am His.

> ***You*** *are sealed by the Holy Spirit of promise.* ***Your*** *standing is not up for renegotiation. The enemy cannot break what God stamped.* ***You*** *are His — permanently.*

1. Where have you been living like your standing with God is fragile — like one bad week could change your position? Be honest about what that looks like practically.

2. What does the enemy most often accuse you of? Write it down. Then write the seal-based response, not based on your performance, but based on what God has declared.

3. What would change in how you approach God this week if you fully believed your standing was sealed — that stumbling does not revoke your access, and accusation has no jurisdiction over what He has settled?

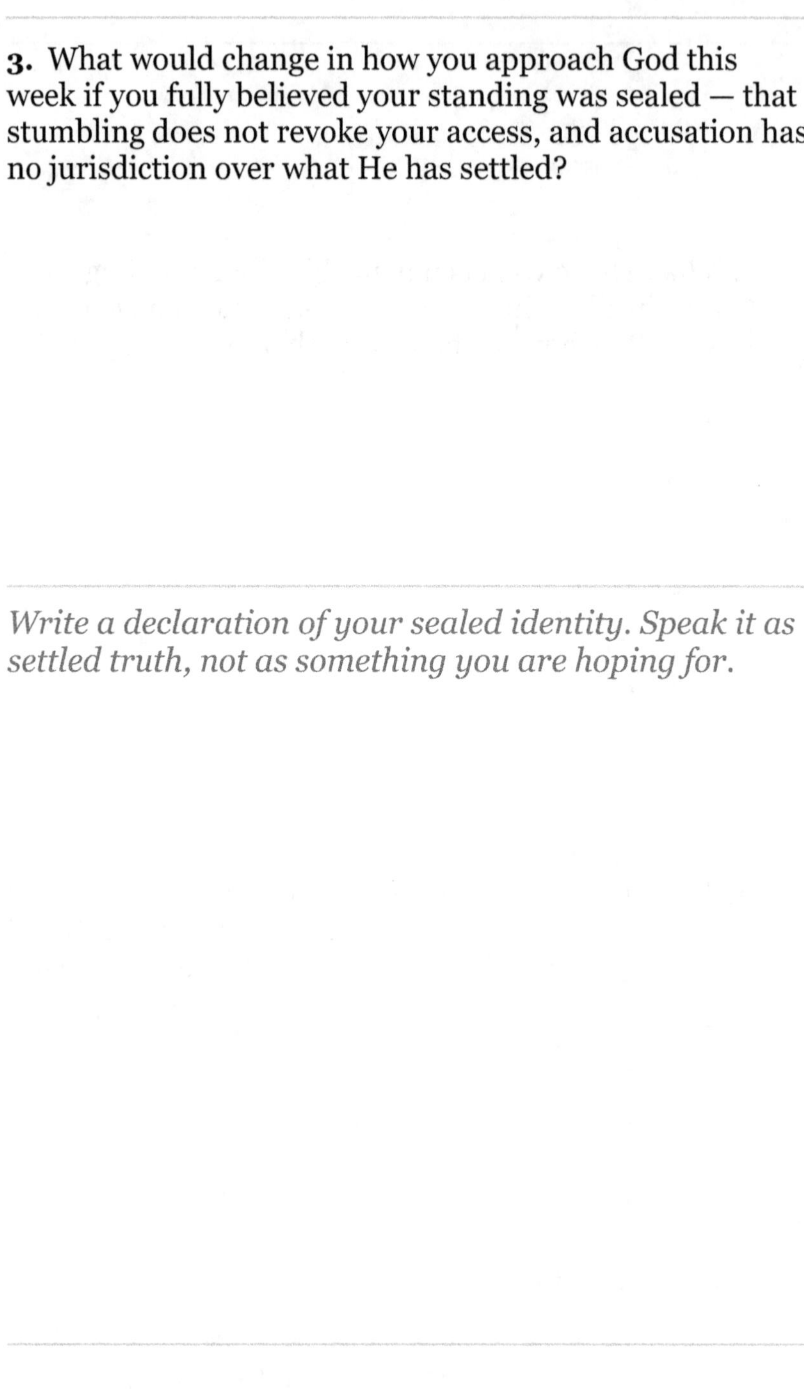

Write a declaration of your sealed identity. Speak it as settled truth, not as something you are hoping for.

"And they overcame him by the blood of the Lamb and by the word of their testimony."

— Revelation 12:11 (NKJV)

Pray to Encourage Yourself

Father,

I have been treating something You made permanent as though it were provisional. I have been living under the shadow of what the accuser says rather than standing on what You declared. Your Word says I was sealed with the Holy Spirit of promise. That seal is not based on my performance. It is based on Your grace and Your choice and the blood of Your Son. Forgive me for the times I retreated from You after stumbling, as though the stumble had changed my standing. Forgive me for giving the enemy's accusations more authority than Your Word. Today I declare what is true: I am sealed. I am Yours. Nothing in all of creation can separate me from Your love. My standing is not fragile. It is settled. I receive that rest today. In Jesus' name, Amen.

CHAPTER 12

Placed, Not Stuck

Where God has you is not accidental

> **What if the season you have been calling 'stuck' is actually the most intentional placement of your life so far?**

I know that question might be landing hard for some of you. Because the season you are in right now may feel anything but intentional. It may feel like everything slowed down when it should be speeding up. It may feel like you have been in the same place for so long that the idea of divine purpose starts to feel like something people say to make you feel better about a situation that is actually just frustrating.

I hear that. And I am not going to paper over it with easy answers.

But I am going to ask you to stay with me, because I believe that the distinction between being stuck and being placed is one of the most identity-altering shifts you can make.

What Stuck Feels Like vs. What Placed Means

Stuck is a word that carries hopelessness with it. It implies that progress has been arrested, that something has gone wrong, that you should be somewhere else by now. Stuck is passive. Stuck is waiting for something external to change before life can resume.

Placed is a completely different word. Placed implies intentionality. Placed implies that someone with authority and purpose made a decision about your location. Placed means positioned, by someone who knows what they are doing and why.

When you are stuck, every day in the same season feels like loss. When you are placed, every day in the same season is potentially purposeful.

Same season. Completely different frame. And the frame is not denial...it is theology. It is what you actually believe about whether God is sovereign over the coordinates of your life.

> *"And He has made from one blood every nation of men to dwell on all the face of the earth, and has determined their preappointed times and the boundaries of their dwellings."* — **Acts 17:26 (NKJV)**

Preappointed times. Determined boundaries. These are not casual words. Your time, the specific moment in history you occupy, was determined. Your place, the specific context you inhabit, was determined. You are not randomly located in history. You are positioned.

THE WORD: **Moed (moh-AYD)**
Appointed time, set season — God's deliberate divine scheduling.
The Hebrew calendar is built on moadim — appointed times. God's interaction with humanity has always been scheduled with precision. Your current season is not a scheduling error. It is a moed — an appointed time that God determined before you arrived in it.

Esther's Palace

For such a time as this.

Esther's presence in that palace, in that season, in that specific moment of crisis, was not accidental. She had been placed. Not by the king who chose her for his court. By the God who positioned her before the crisis arrived so that when the crisis came, she would be exactly where she needed to be to be part of the answer.

But here is what I want you to notice: Esther could not see any of this from inside her placement. From inside the palace, what she saw was constraint, risk, and the weight of a demand she had not signed up for.

Your placement may look like limitation from the inside. The job that feels too small. The city that feels too familiar. The season that has been going on longer than you planned.

But who knows whether you have come to this place for such a time as this?

THE WORD: **Natah (nah-TAH)**

To plant, to stretch out, to pitch — the intentional establishment of something in a specific location.

God does not accidentally place people any more than a farmer accidentally plants seeds. Natah describes deliberate, purposeful positioning. When God places you somewhere, He has considered the soil, the season, and what He expects to grow. You are not randomly located. You are deliberately planted.

Roots Before Branches

When a tree is young, the most significant growth is the growth you cannot see. Before the branches spread wide. Before the leaves come in full. Before the tree produces anything visible, the roots are going deep. The roots are extending further into the earth, securing themselves, building the infrastructure that will eventually support everything the tree is meant to produce.

If you evaluated that young tree from the outside, measuring only visible progress, you would conclude nothing is happening. But underground, where no one is watching, the most important work of the tree's life is underway.

Depth before width. Roots before branches. Foundation before height.

Some of you are in a root season right now. And the enemy has been feeding you a story about how nothing is happening, how you should be further. But what he is not telling you is that what God is building underground in this season is the only thing that will sustain what He wants to build above ground in the next one.

Your placement season is building roots. That is not nothing. That is everything.

The invitation of placement is not passivity. It is full presence.

Wherever God has placed you right now is the fullest expression of your current assignment. The people in your building. The community in your neighborhood. The relationships in your immediate circle. The unremarkable daily rhythms of your actual life. These are not the waiting room for the real thing. This is the real thing.

You are not stuck. You are planted.

And planted things grow.

> **You** are not stuck. **You** are placed. God determined your appointed time and the boundaries of your season with intention. Planted things grow — in His time, from His purpose.

Take your time with these. Write honestly. This is your book.

1. What season of your life have you been calling 'stuck'? Write an honest description of what that season looks like from the inside.

2. Now write what that same season might look like if you were fully convinced you were placed rather than trapped. What would you do differently? What would you invest in that you have been holding back from?

3. The Esther question: Who knows whether you have come to your current location for such a time as this? Sit with that and write what you sense God might be building or positioning you for through this very season.

Write a letter to your current season. Acknowledge it honestly. Then release the stuck interpretation and receive the placed one.

Father,

I want to be honest with You about the tension I have been living in. There are seasons, and this may be one of them, when where I am does not feel like where I am supposed to be. When the vision You placed in me and the reality I am living in feel far apart. When waiting feels like being forgotten. And today I choose to lay that interpretation down and receive something different. I choose to believe that You marked out my appointed time with intention. That You placed me here, in this season, in this place, in these relationships, with purpose. Help me show up fully to this season. Help me invest in the present rather than half-living it while I wait for the next thing. Help me trust that the roots You are building in me right now are exactly what the branches will need. I am planted. Not stuck. I receive that today. In Jesus' name, Amen.

WALKING IN YOUR TRUE NAME

"Identity is not a destination. It is a daily decision."

CHAPTER 13

A Friend of God

You were not saved just to serve Him... oohhh.. you were invited close

---

> **Is your relationship with God characterized more by duty than by closeness? And when did those two things become the same thing to you?**

I want to ask you something that might feel like an unusual question for a book about identity. But I think it might be the most important question in Part Five.

Do you actually know God? Not know about Him. Not know His word, His ways, His doctrines, His requirements. Know Him. Personally. The way you know someone you have spent real time with, been honest with, listened to, argued with, been changed by.

Because there is a version of Christian life that can be lived entirely on the surface. You can attend every service, read every scripture, serve in every ministry, check every religious box, and never actually develop a genuine relationship with the God you are doing all of it for.

You can be deeply busy for God without being deeply known by God. And you can spend years wondering why something feels hollow in the middle of all that activity.

This chapter is about that hollow place. And about the truth that was meant to fill it.

What Jesus Said at the Table

> *"No longer do I call you servants, for a servant does not know what his master is doing; but I have called you friends, for all things that I heard from My Father I have made known to you."* — **John 15:15 (NKJV)**

Read that again and let the weight of it land.

Jesus changed the category. Not gradually. Not eventually. Right there at the table, with the authority of the One who was about to complete the work of redemption, He said: I am changing how I identify you. Not servants. Friends.

In the culture of that day, this was not a casual upgrade. In Jewish religious culture, the distance between God and human beings was built into the architecture. The Temple system communicated it clearly: outer court, inner court, Holy of Holies, each zone representing a diminished level of access.

And then Jesus gathered twelve ordinary people at an ordinary table and said: I call you friends.

That sentence dismantled the entire structure of religious distance in one breath.

The Difference Between a Servant and a Friend

Jesus gives us the distinction Himself, and it is precise: a servant does not know what his master is doing. A friend does.

A servant operates on instructions. They are told what to do and they do it. The master's heart, the master's reasoning, the master's bigger picture, none of that is shared with a servant.

A friend is let into the inner thinking. A friend is trusted with the heart, not just the task. A friend is someone you share your plans with, your hopes, your concerns, your reasoning, not because they need to know to do their job, but because the relationship itself is the point.

And Jesus says: I have made known to you all things that I heard from My Father. He pulled His disciples into it. He taught them. He explained. He answered questions. He let them see Him in the private moments.

That is not how you treat servants. That is how you treat friends.

And He is treating you the same way.

THE WORD: **Re'a (ray-AH)**
Friend, companion, intimate — one you are genuinely close to.
Exodus 33:11 says God spoke to Moses face to face, as a man speaks to his re'a — his friend. This is peer language. Companion language. The kind of closeness that is built over time through honest, present, unhurried relationship. God did not invent friendship with humanity at the Last Supper. He had been doing it from the beginning.

Religion Can Substitute for Relationship

Religious activity can substitute for genuine relationship with God. And the substitution is so seamless that you can go years without recognizing it.

I grew up in a household where faith was central. I knew the language before I knew the reality behind it. I could speak about God with fluency and confidence and have nothing genuine happening in the private place between me and Him. I was performing faith in a house full of real faith, and for a long time I could not tell the difference.

What finally forced the distinction was a season when the performance stopped working. When the external structures fell away and all that was left was me and a God I knew a great deal about but had not yet fully known.

That is when I discovered what the friendship Jesus was describing in John 15 actually felt like. Not because I was spiritual enough to produce it. But because I was finally desperate enough to stop substituting for it.

And what I found on the other side of that honesty changed everything.

THE WORD: **Ahav (ah-HAHV)**

To love, to be a friend, to have deep affection — covenant love.
Ahav is the word behind God's love for His people throughout the Old Testament. It is not the casual affection of someone who finds you pleasant. It is covenant love — the kind that makes a binding commitment, that does not withdraw when things get hard, that stays present through seasons that would cause lesser love to leave. God's friendship with you is ahav. It was never casual.

What Friendship Does to Your Identity

When you spend real time with Someone who knows you completely and loves you without condition, something changes at the level of how you see yourself. The shame that drove you into hiding loses its power. The performance falls away. The walls start to come down.

When you are the friend of God, when that is not just theological language but something you have actually experienced in the private place, you carry something into every room you enter that people can feel without being able to name. A settledness. A groundedness. A quiet confidence that is not performing certainty but simply has it.

That is what identity rooted in genuine friendship with God produces. Not arrogance. Not performance. Just the quiet, unshakeable knowing of someone who has been with Someone.

You are not just God's worker. You are not just His servant. You are not just a beneficiary of His grace.

You are His friend. He chose you as His friend before you knew to want it. And the invitation He extended in that upper room is still standing.

Come close. Be known. Be honest. Stay.

> **You** are not just saved. **You** are invited close. Not a servant performing for approval — a friend. Known fully, loved without condition, invited into the inner room.

Take your time with these. Write honestly. This is your book.

1. Be honest: Has your relationship with God been more transactional or relational? What does that look like specifically in how you pray, how you approach Him after you stumble, how present you are with Him day to day?

2. Have you been substituting religious activity for genuine relationship with God? Where has the busyness been covering the hollow place?

3. What would it look like to bring the real version of yourself to God today — not the cleaned-up version, not the performing version, but the actual you? Write what that conversation would sound like.

Write a letter to God as a friend — honest, unfiltered, present. Not a prayer list. A conversation.

"Abraham believed God, and it was accounted to him for righteousness. And he was called the friend of God."

— **James 2:23 (NKJV)**

Talk to your Father..

Father,

I want to receive this today in a way I may not have before. You are not waiting at the end of a long list of requirements I have to meet before I can approach You. You are close. You have always been close. And You are calling me friend.I confess the times I turned our relationship into performance. The times I came to You with the managed version of myself. The times I let activity substitute for intimacy.Today I choose differently. I come as I am, the full version, the real version. I want the friendship You are offering. Not just the salvation. Not just the title. The actual friendship, daily, honest, transforming.Teach me how to stay close. I am Yours. And You are mine.In Jesus' name, Amen.

CHAPTER 14

God's Workmanship in Motion

Identity without action is incomplete

> *After everything you have received in this book — what are you going to do with it?*

I want to ask that question plainly and without apology, because we have arrived at the point in this journey where receiving is not enough anymore.

You can know that you are chosen. You can know that you are sealed, accepted, placed, the friend of God, His crafted poem. You can carry every one of those truths in your head and be able to articulate them with precision and conviction.

And then you can walk out the door and continue living exactly the same way you were living before any of it landed.

Because knowledge, by itself, does not transform. It is knowledge acted upon, truth received deeply enough that it actually changes your choices, your posture, your use of the gifts God gave you, your willingness to step into the spaces He opens, that is what transformation looks like from the outside.

This chapter is about that step. The step from knowing to doing. From identity received to identity expressed. From

God's workmanship sitting still to God's workmanship in motion.

The Parable That Makes Us Uncomfortable

Matthew 25:14-30 is the parable of the talents. You have heard it. And because you have heard it enough times, there is a real danger that you have become inoculated against it.

The master leaves. He distributes portions to three servants. The first two go immediately and multiply what they were given. The third, and here is the part worth sitting inside, digs a hole and buries the talent.

He does not spend it on himself. He does not gamble it away. He keeps it. He preserves it. He returns it to the master exactly as it was given, undiminished and intact.

And the master's response is severe.

> *"But his lord answered and said to him, 'You wicked and lazy servant... you ought to have deposited my money with the bankers, and at my coming I would have received back my own with interest.'"* — Matthew 25:26-27 (NKJV)

Wicked and lazy. Those are not the words you use for someone who tried and failed. They are the words for someone who did not try. Who chose safety over faithfulness.

That servant had a gift. It was real. It was given intentionally. And he buried it.

The question before you now is: what have you been burying?

THE WORD: **Charisma (kha-RISS-mah)**

Grace-gift — a gift given freely through God's favor, not earned.
Every gift you carry is charisma — an expression of God's
grace poured into you in a specific form, to flow through you
to others. You did not earn it. You cannot lose it through
failure. But you can bury it through fear. And a buried gift
does not accomplish what it was placed in you to accomplish.

False Humility Is a Real Thing

It sounds like this: I don't want to be seen. I'm not sure
I'm ready. There are people more qualified than me. I'll
step out when I feel more prepared.

And that sounds humble. It sounds like the spiritually
responsible thing.

But I want to offer you a different lens. Because
sometimes what looks like humility is actually fear
wearing spiritual clothing. True humility uses the gift
freely and gives all credit to the One who provided it. It is
false humility, rooted in unhealed insecurity and
unresolved identity questions, that buries the gift and calls
the burying wisdom.

I am not asking you to perform a gift you do not have. I
am asking you to stop hiding the one you do.

Someone Is Waiting

There is someone who is waiting for what God put in you.

Not waiting in the abstract. Waiting specifically. Someone
whose path is going to cross yours, or already has, who
needs the exact combination of story, gift, perspective,
and presence that only you carry. Someone who will hear

something from you that they have not been able to receive from anyone else, because the way God made you is the specific angle of light that will reach them.

That person does not need the polished, platform-ready, fully-formed version of you. They need the real one.

Someone is waiting for the book you have not written yet.

Someone is waiting for the conversation you have been too afraid to have.

Someone is waiting for the song that is still inside you.

Someone is waiting for the version of you that has finally decided to show up fully.

Do not make them wait any longer.

*God's workmanship in **you** was never meant to sit still. Someone is waiting for what He placed in **you**. Stop burying it. Step out.*

Take your time with these. Write honestly. This is your book.

1. What gift have you been burying? Name it specifically. How long have you been burying it, and what has the burying cost you and the people who needed it?

2. Where has false humility been functioning in your life — fear dressed up in spiritual language? What would true humility look like instead?

3. Who specifically might be waiting for what God put in you? Write a name if one comes to mind. Then write what the first step of showing up for them would actually look like.

Write a commitment to God about what you are going to stop burying and start using. Make it specific. Make it this week, not someday.

"As each one has received a gift, minister it to one another, as good stewards of the manifold grace of God."

— 1 Peter 4:10 (NKJV)

PRAY THIS

Father,

I have done a lot of receiving in this book. I have received truth about who I am. I have received healing from things that needed to be healed. And today, at this chapter, I make a commitment to You.I will use what You gave me.I will stop burying the gift because I am afraid of what will happen if I actually invest it. I will stop waiting for the perfect moment, the perfect version of myself, the perfect season. I will begin, imperfectly, faithfully, with what I have from where I am.Show me specifically what using the gift looks like in this season. Show me the people You intend for me to serve. Give me the courage to walk through the doors You have opened that I have been standing in front of.Let my identity be in motion. Let the workmanship You invested in me be visible in the world, not for my glory, but for Yours. And for the people who are waiting for what You put in me. Here I am. Use me. In Jesus' name, Amen.

CHAPTER 15

Salt and Light

You don't need a platform. You need presence.

> *What if the most significant assignment God ever gave you is not the one you are waiting for, but the one happening in the ordinary places you walk through every single day?*

> *"You are the salt of the earth... You are the light of the world." —* Matthew 5:13-14 (NKJV)

Are. Present tense. Not: you will be if you achieve enough. Not: you could be if you step up. Not: you would be if you were more consistent.

You are. Right now. Today. In this season. In this body. In this city. In this job. In the ordinary, unremarkable, not-yet-platform moments of your actual life.

This is not future identity. This is present reality. And Jesus did not say it as an aspiration. He said it as a declaration. He was not inviting them to become something. He was naming what they already were.

That is your identity too. Not what you are working toward. What you already are.

Why Salt? The Covenant Behind the Image

In our culture, salt is a seasoning. It sits on a table and adds flavor to food. That is a deeply diminished version of what salt meant in the ancient world.

Salt in the ancient Near East was one of the most valuable substances known to human civilization. It preserved food in a world with no refrigeration. It was used in purification rituals. It was a medium of trade. And crucially for the people Jesus was speaking to, salt had profound covenantal significance.

> *"It is a covenant of salt forever before the Lord with you and your descendants with you."* — **Numbers 18:19 (NKJV)**

A covenant of salt meant: this is unbreakable. This is without end. This is backed by the character of God Himself.

So when Jesus calls you the salt of the earth, He is not saying you add a little flavor to life. He is saying you carry covenant. You carry the preserving, purifying, binding presence of God into every environment you enter. Your presence is not decorative. It is covenantal.

Salt preserves. Your presence in environments slows the moral and spiritual decay that happens when the covenant community is absent.

Salt enhances. Your presence brings out what is true, what is good, what is possible in the people and places around you.

Salt purifies. Your presence carries a kind of holy pressure that makes certain things uncomfortable in a way that produces change rather than damage.

Salt — used in covenant ratification, purification, and preservation.

Leviticus 2:13 says: with all your offerings you shall offer salt. Salt was not optional in Israel's worship. It was the marker of covenant permanence. When Jesus calls you melach — salt — He is calling you a covenant carrier. You bring the permanent, purifying presence of God into every space you occupy.

You Are the Light of the World

Light works differently than salt. Light does not need to touch something to affect it. Light changes the environment simply by being present in it. Darkness is not an entity that resists light. Darkness is the absence of light. And the moment light appears, darkness does not fight back. It simply retreats.

Your identity as light means that your presence changes environments not primarily through what you say or do, but through what you carry.

> *"Nor do they light a lamp and put it under a basket, but on a lampstand, and it gives light to all who are in the house. Let your light so shine before men, that they may see your good works and glorify your Father in heaven."* — Matthew 5:15-16 (NKJV)

The lamp has one job. Shine.

Do not cover yourself. Do not apologize for taking up space. Do not shrink because the room seems too dark or too large or too indifferent to what you carry.

Shine.

Your Ordinary Life Is the Assignment

The workplace where nobody knows you follow Jesus, that is not a problem to be solved by getting a job at a ministry. That is an assignment. You are the only salt and light in that particular room, with access to those particular people, at this particular moment in their lives.

The neighborhood where you have lived for years but barely know anyone, that is an invitation. Not an indictment of your evangelism. An invitation to actually be present in the place God placed you.

The relationship where someone is watching how you handle the hard things, deciding whether the God you talk about is real, that is a ministry moment. Not when you are polished and prepared. Right now, in the ordinary, unscripted, real version of your life.

You do not need a bigger platform to be salt and light. You need to stop being ashamed of the platform you already have.

Shine where you are. That is enough. That has always been enough.

> ***You*** *are the salt of the earth.* ***You*** *are the light of the world. Present tense. Right now. In the ordinary places.* ***You*** *don't need a bigger platform.* ***You*** *need presence.*

GOING DEEPER

Take your time with these. Write honestly. This is your book.

1. List your five most regular environments — work, home, neighborhood, community. In each one, write specifically what being salt (preserving, enhancing, purifying) looks like. Not in theory. In your actual life.

2. Have you been covering your light — shrinking, blending in, apologizing for what you carry? Where specifically has that been happening and why?

3. Who in your immediate world is watching how you handle the hard things and deciding whether the God you talk about is real? Write their name and what being present to them actually looks like this week.

A WORD TO CARRY

"Let your light so shine before men, that they may see your good works and glorify your Father in heaven."

— **Matthew 5:16 (NKJV)**

Father,

You called me salt and light before I ever earned it. Thank You for that. Thank You that this identity is not waiting for me to achieve a certain level or reach a certain platform or develop a certain polish.Forgive me for the times I have covered the light. For the times I have diluted the salt by trying to blend in instead of standing distinct. For treating my ordinary environments as less than they are, when they are exactly where You placed me on purpose.Today I receive the assignment: show up, be present, and let what lives in me affect what is around me. I don't need to make announcements. I just need to be who You said I am, in every room You place me in.Shine through me today.In Jesus' name, Amen.

CHAPTER 16

Living From Identity, Not Chasing It

The name you answer to is the life you live.

> **What if the life you have been trying to build... was supposed to flow from who you already are?**

Not something you earn. Not something you prove. Not something you chase.

Something you live from.

Sit with that.

Because most people spend their entire lives trying to become someone God already said they were. Trying to achieve what was already given. Trying to prove what was already settled. Trying to earn what was already spoken over them before they drew their first breath.

And the result?

Exhaustion. Confusion. A life that looks full on the outside but feels unstable on the inside.

Not because you are doing too little.

Because you are building from the wrong place.

This is the chapter where that changes.

This Entire Book Has Been About One Thing

Every chapter you just read, every label we named, every false foundation we dismantled, every truth we laid down in its place, was building toward this single shift.

Returning to your real name.

Not the name life gave you. Not the name pain gave you. Not the name people wrote on you in seasons when they were working with incomplete information. Not the name you gave yourself on your worst day.

The name God wrote.

Before you were born. Before you performed. Before you succeeded or failed. Before anyone else had a pen.

You do not become chosen. You were chosen.

You do not become accepted. You were made accepted.

You do not become enough. You have been complete in Him from the moment you believed.

The problem was never your identity.

The problem was the agreement.

You had the right foundation the whole time. You just kept agreeing with the wrong voice about what was standing on it.

The Real Difference Between Chasing and Living From

Chasing identity is future-tense and exhausting. It sounds like: one day I will finally know who I am. One day I will feel secure enough to stop second-guessing myself. One day I will walk into rooms without calculating how I am being perceived. One day I will stop shrinking. One day I will believe what God says about me.

One day. One day. One day.

But one day never comes. Because chasing is a posture, not a pace. You can speed up and still be chasing. You can work harder and still be chasing. You can go to more conferences, read more books, get more prayer, check more spiritual boxes, and still be chasing.

Because chasing is not about effort. It is about foundation.

Living from identity is present-tense and restful. It sounds like: this is already true. I receive it. I walk in it today. I make decisions from this foundation today. I filter what the world says through what God has already declared. I respond to difficulty from a settled place. Not one day. Now.

The difference is not between active and passive. Both people are moving. Both are working. Both are serving.

The difference is where the work is coming from.

One is building their identity. The other is expressing it.

One is striving to become something. The other is releasing what was already placed inside them.

Same life. Completely different experience.

> *"For in Him dwells all the fullness of the Godhead bodily; and you are complete in Him, who is the head of all principality and power."* — Colossians 2:9-10 (NKJV)

Complete. Not becoming complete. Not almost complete. Not complete pending further spiritual development.

Complete. In Him. Right now.

The issue is never that the identity is unavailable. The issue is agreement. You can have everything God has provided and still live beneath it because you have not yet agreed with it at the level that changes your behavior.

This book was never about giving you new information. It was about changing your agreement.

Where Most People Miss It

Most people read a book like this, feel genuinely moved, highlight passages, pray the prayers, mean every word, and then go right back to living the same way.

Still chasing. Still proving. Still adjusting their presentation based on who is in the room. Still shrinking when they should be standing. Still answering to names God never gave them.

Not because they did not receive the truth. Because information does not change identity.

Agreement does.

You can know that you are chosen and still live like you are auditioning.

You can know that you are accepted and still approach God like a guest who is nervous about overstaying their welcome.

You can know that you are sealed and still collapse under the weight of the enemy's accusations.

Knowing and agreeing are two different things. And until the knowing drops from your head into your actual daily choices, until it starts showing up in how you walk into rooms, how you respond to criticism, how you handle seasons of invisibility, how you love people who cannot give you anything in return, it is still just information.

God is not after your information. He is after your agreement.

> **You cannot say 'God chose me' and still live like you have to prove yourself. At some point, you have to choose.**

So Here Is The Question

Not what did you highlight in this book.

Not what sounded true when you read it.

Not what you plan to come back to someday.

What name are you going to answer to now?

Because you cannot live in two identities at the same time. You cannot say God chose me and still live like you have to earn your place. You cannot say I am accepted and still shrink in rooms you were called to walk into. You cannot say I am His and still let people rename you every time they misunderstand you or overlook you or decide you are too much.

At some point, you have to choose.

Not when life gets easier. Not when people finally see you correctly. Not when your circumstances catch up to your calling. Not when you feel more spiritually prepared than you do right now.

Right here. Right now.

I will no longer answer to what God never said.

That is the decision this whole book has been building toward. And you are the only one who can make it.

What Living From Identity Actually Looks Like

Living from identity does not mean your life suddenly becomes easy. It does not mean you stop feeling fear or doubt or the pull of old habits. It does not mean the labels stop coming. They will keep coming. People will keep projecting. Seasons will keep trying to define you.

What changes is not what comes at you.

What changes is what you are standing on when it arrives.

It looks like showing up without shrinking — walking into rooms that used to make you perform with a quiet settledness instead. Not loudness. Not bravado. Just not needing the room's approval to know why you are there.

It looks like speaking without filtering truth through fear, saying the true thing even when the true thing is not the crowd-pleasing thing, because your standing is not contingent on the response.

It looks like resting without guilt, taking a Sabbath and not spending it fighting the low-grade anxiety that you should be producing something. Because your worth is not in your output.

It looks like obeying without needing applause, being faithful in private with the same quality of effort you bring when someone is watching. Because the Father who sees in secret is the audience that matters.

It looks like letting God define you even when people do not understand you, being misread, mischaracterized, or overlooked and not needing to correct the record.

It looks like peace. Not the peace that comes from everything going well. The peace that passes understanding. The peace that is available in the middle of the storm because your identity is not in the weather.

The Lie and The Truth

The lie says: once I fix the broken places, I will be enough.

Once I perform consistently, I will earn my place.

Once people finally see me correctly, I will feel secure.

Once the season changes, I will start living the life I was made for.

The lie always puts your identity just out of reach. Just past the next achievement. Just past the next healing. Just past the next season.

But here is the truth.

Because you are already His, you can grow without fear. You do not have to perform your way into security. You do not have to fix yourself into acceptability. You do not have to wait for the right circumstances to start being fully who God made you.

Growth happens from a settled foundation, not toward one.

You are not growing into your identity. You are growing from it.

Say It Plain

So say it. Out loud. Let your voice be the last thing you hear agreeing with God before you close this book.

I am not what happened to me.

I am not what people called me.

I am not what I did on my worst day or failed to do on my best one.

I am not the sum of my seasons.

I am not the weight of my wounds.

I am who God said.

And what He said... still stands.

Your Next Step Is Not Someday

You have read the truth. Every chapter has done its work. The labels have been named. The foundations have been examined. The declarations have been spoken.

Now live it.

Not tomorrow. Not when you feel ready. Not when life cooperates. Not when the old voices quiet down on their own.

Now. With what you have. From where you are standing. With the exact version of yourself that finished this book.

When the thought comes that says you are not enough, answer it. Out loud. With what you know.

When the old label shows up like it owns something, reject it. Not politely. Firmly. It does not live here anymore.

When fear tries to rename you in the middle of the obedient step, stand. The fear is not information about your identity. It is just noise.

When comparison pulls at you in rooms full of gifted people, let it go. You are not in their lane. You are in yours.

When the season is hidden and nobody is watching and faithfulness feels thankless, remember. El Roi sees. The Father who sees in secret does not forget what He sees.

Identity is not something you visit. It is not a truth you borrow on good days and return when things get hard.

It is something you live from. Every single day. As a daily decision, a daily agreement, a daily choice to return to the foundation when everything else is trying to relocate you.

A Final Word From Me to You

You made it to the end of this book. And I do not say that casually, because I know what this kind of book asks of you. It asks you to look at things you have been avoiding. To sit with discomfort long enough for God to do something with it. To receive truths that felt almost too good to be true and hold them long enough to let them actually land.

I am proud of you for that. Really. It takes something to stay with this kind of work.

This was not about making you feel better. This was about making you free.

There is a difference. Feeling better is temporary. Freedom is foundational. It comes from knowing whose you are so deeply that what happens around you cannot relocate what is settled inside you.

That is what I want for you. Not a good day. A free life.

You are not the labels. You never were.

You are God's daughter. His son. His workmanship. His poem. His friend. His chosen, known, accepted, sealed, placed, complete child.

That was true before you opened this book. It will be true long after you put it down.

The unveiling has happened. Now live like what is underneath is real.

Because it is.

Keep your identity in check.

It's a great day to have a great day.
And don't let nobody steal your joy today.

> **The name you answer to is the life you live. So choose your name wisely.**

1. Which of the identity truths in this book hit you the hardest? What did it reveal about what you had been believing about yourself before you read it?

2. What specific agreement have you been making with a lie that this book helped you identify? Write the lie, then write God's word over it.

3. What is one concrete, specific way you will actively live from identity, not chase it, starting this week? Not someday. This week.

4. Write a declaration beginning with: I am... Pull from every chapter. Write who God says you are. Make it yours.

Father, thank You. Thank You for the truth You revealed in these pages. Thank You for every label that was named, every lie that was exposed, and every part of their identity that was restored or revealed for the first time.

I pray that they receive every truth that was declared in this book. Not just for a moment, but as a daily way of living. Let this not be information they heard, but truth they walk in.

Remind them that they are not who their past said they were. They are not who pain tried to define them as. They are not what anyone called them while operating with incomplete understanding.

They are who You said they are. Chosen. Known. Accepted. Sealed. Placed. Your workmanship. Your friend. Salt and light. Complete in You. And what You said still stands.

When they feel themselves drifting back to old agreements, bring them back quickly. Let Your Word be louder than every other voice. Let what You established hold firm, even when everything around them feels uncertain.

Let this truth take root. Let it grow. Let it shape how they think, how they move, and how they live. They are Yours. They always have been.

And I thank You that they will walk in that truth with clarity, confidence, and conviction. In Jesus' name, Amen.

Speak each declaration out loud. Then write it in your own hand.

Let every word land. Let your voice agree with what God already declared.

I am who God says I am.

I am CHOSEN — before the foundation of the world, with full knowledge.

I am KNOWN — fully, intimately, and without exception.

I am ACCEPTED — not tolerated. Not on probation. I am Beloved.

I am SEALED — by the Holy Spirit of promise. Nothing can separate me.

I am PLACED — not stuck. My appointed time was determined with purpose.

I am a FRIEND OF GOD — not a servant performing for approval.

I am His WORKMANSHIP — His poem. Crafted with intention. Not random.

**I am SALT AND LIGHT — covenant carrier,
world-changer, right where I am.**

**I am COMPLETE in Him. Not working toward it.
Living from it. Now.**

I will not go back.

Signature: _______________________________________

Date: _______________

IDENTITY DIRECTORY

Come back here when the lies get loud. When the labels try to reattach. When you forget. God's Word does not expire and neither does what it declares over you.

Bookmark it. Dog-ear it. Write in the margins. This is not a library book.

I AM CHOSEN

Ephesians 1:4 (NKJV)	*"He chose us in Him before the foundation of the world."* Chosen before time began. Not because of what I have done. Because of who He is.
John 15:16 (NKJV)	*"You did not choose Me, but I chose you and appointed you."* God made the first move. My belonging to Him was His idea before it was mine.

I AM KNOWN

Psalm 139:1-3	*"O Lord, You have searched me and known me."*

| (NKJV) | God does not know about me. He knows me. Every ordinary moment. Every hidden season. |

| **Genesis 16:13** (NKJV) | *"She called the name of the Lord, You-Are-the-God-Who-Sees."* El Roi sees me in the wilderness too. Not just when I am performing. Always. |

I AM ACCEPTED

| **Ephesians 1:6** (NKJV) | *"He made us accepted in the Beloved."* Not on probation. Not tolerated. Made accepted, past tense, complete, not pending review. |

| **Romans 8:1** (NKJV) | *"There is therefore now no condemnation to those who are in Christ Jesus."* Conviction leads me back to God. Condemnation is not from Him. I run toward Him, not away. |

I AM SEALED

| **Ephesians 1:13** (NKJV) | *"Having believed, you were sealed with the Holy Spirit of promise."* My standing is not fragile. The seal is not based on my performance. It cannot be broken. |

Romans 8:38-39 (NKJV)	*"Neither death nor life... shall be able to separate us from the love of God."* Nothing in all creation can separate me from God's love. Not this season. Not this failure. Nothing.

I AM PLACED

Acts 17:26 (NKJV)	*"He has determined their preappointed times and the boundaries of their dwellings."* I am not stuck. I am placed. My season was not a scheduling error.
Jeremiah 29:11 (NKJV)	*"For I know the plans I have for you... plans for welfare and not for evil."* The waiting is preparation, not punishment. His plans have not changed.

I AM HIS WORKMANSHIP

Ephesians 2:10 (NKJV)	*"For we are His workmanship, created in Christ Jesus for good works."* God's poem. Crafted with intention. Nothing about how He made me is accidental.

<table>
<tr><td>Colossians 2:10
(NKJV)</td><td>"You are complete in Him."
Complete in Christ right now. Not when I achieve more. Not when I heal more. Now.</td></tr>
</table>

I AM A FRIEND OF GOD

<table>
<tr><td>John 15:15
(NKJV)</td><td>"I have called you friends, for all things that I heard from My Father I have made known to you."
Not just saved. Invited close. He shares His heart with me, not just His assignments.</td></tr>
</table>

I AM SALT AND LIGHT

<table>
<tr><td>Matthew 5:13-14
(NKJV)</td><td>"You are the salt of the earth... You are the light of the world."
Present tense. Right now. In this season, this room, this ordinary Tuesday.</td></tr>
</table>

> **When the lies get loud, come back here. This is what God said. And God does not take it back.**

IDENTITY

A Gospel • R&B Experience

The album companion to this book, music that carries the same truth into your every day. Streaming on ALL Platforms NOW!

Scan QR Code Below to Check Out The Merch Store

- Faith-based Apparel
- Journals
- Coloring Books
- Ebooks & More.

www.alowemerch.com

JOIN US

**A night of worship, truth, and real community.
Not performance. Not pressure. Just presence.**

EVERY 3RD SUNDAY
5:00 PM
Guiding Light Church
Birmingham, Alabama

Scan for details

TheGatheringBHam.com
Come as you are.
Everyone is welcome.

Before she taught identity, she had to find hers.

ALowe McCants knows what it feels like to carry strength that looks right on the outside but feels heavy on the inside. To be capable, dependable, and gifted... yet still wrestle with the quiet question, *"Who am I when I am not performing?"*

That question changed everything.

What began as a personal search became a clear assignment.

Today, ALowe is a book coach, ghostwriter, youth pastor, speaker, songwriter, and AI specialist committed to helping people see themselves the way God sees them. Her teaching is direct, grounded in Scripture, and shaped by real life. She does not deal in surface motivation. She helps people confront what has been misplaced so they can finally live from what is true.

Her work has helped authors find their voice, believers find their footing, and everyday people break free from pressure, comparison, and identity built on performance.

She is the author of *The Triumph Playbook: Strategies for Overcoming Darkness and Living in the Light* and the voice behind **"Great Day,"** a weekday devotional that reaches thousands each morning with clarity, conviction, and encouragement. Her message is simple but steady: when you start with Jesus, you do not have to search for direction... you walk in it.

ALowe also creates faith-based journals, apparel, and resources designed to make identity practical. Not just something you read. Something you live.

She lives in Birmingham with her husband Matt and their son Sam, building a life rooted in faith, family, and the daily decision to live from who God says she is.

Connect with ALowe:
@its.alowe
alowemerch.com
itsalowe.com